Joseph K. Manchester

Northern Son in the South, 1861-1863
His Letters, Family, and Friends

Carol H. Manchester

Joseph K. Manchester
Northern Son in the South, 1861-1863

© 2013 Carol H. Manchester

ISBN 13: 978-1-938883-75-0

All maps courtesy of David Manchester

designed and produced by
Maine Authors Publishing
558 Main Street, Rockland, Maine
www.maineauthorspublishing.com

To the memory of Joseph K. Manchester, the Windham boys,
and to all soldiers, North and South,
who valiantly committed their lives to their principles

CONTENTS

ACKNOWLEDGMENTS

So often authors recognize a very special person near the end of their acknowledgments, but I wish to break with that convention. The letters of David's great uncle Joseph K. Manchester are the genesis of this book, and without our many shared evenings reading, discussing, learning from, and considering them, this book may never have come to fruition. David's exchange of ideas and recommendations, his assistance with research, deciphering, and word suggestions, and his photographic and map drawing contributions have been immeasurably helpful to this project, and this book is as much his as it is mine. To my husband David, for his loving support and involvement, I offer my abiding and heartfelt appreciation.

At the Brown Research Library in Portland, center for collections of the Maine Historical Society since 1822, Jamie Rice set in motion, both figuratively and literally, a journey to locate Joseph. Through her discussion of transport of soldiers' bodies, David and I realized that Arlington Cemetery in Windham likely was *not* Joseph's final resting ground. She led us to the *Roll of Honor*, which in turn brought us to Beaufort National Cemetery in South Carolina. To Jamie Rice and the staff at Brown Research Library, who also helped us in later visits, thank you.

Kay Soldier eagerly and promptly searched the archives of the Windham Historical Society for information and pictures, and much appreciation goes to Kay. Dave Tanguay of WHS similarly deserves my gratitude for providing early Windham photos.

Two Civil War re-enactor units in Maine have been especially helpful in furthering knowledge and grasp of the conflict. Representing Union and Confederate perspectives, the Third Maine Regiment, Company A, and the 15th Alabama, Company G, respectively, provided realism to their encampments and authenticity to the experience by living the camp life of Civil War infantrymen, officers, and officers' wives. In period clothing they speak knowledgeably of field and battle conditions, firearms, rude medical settings, surgeries, and of all matters related to the Civil War. For these men, women, and youths I am appreciative, not only for their improvement of my understanding but also for their respect for and preservation of this defining period in the nation's development.

There are not words proper enough to express how grateful I am to Stephen R. Wise, Ph.D., director of the Parris Island Museum, South Carolina, who so generously gave several hours of his time and scholarship on an October afternoon in 2012 to explain the battles for Battery Wagner in July 1863, to describe Beaufort during the Civil War, its Union occupation and hospitals, to locate General Hospital No. 2 so that I could see the building the next day, and to provide historic photos. Both Stephen Wise and his book *Gate of Hell, Campaign for Charleston Harbor, 1863* were invaluable resources to me.

Another kind and respected individual who greatly assisted understanding of Joseph's probable role in the assault on Fort Wagner on July 18, 1863, is Dana R. MacBean, exhibits curator and cartographer, also at Parris Island Museum. Graciously he provided his time and knowledge; his discussion and the detailed map of the evening battle showing Federal troop movement and Confederate locations brought realism to the battle. Similarly, his map "Federal Siege Operations Against Battery Wagner, Morris Island" from July 10 to September 9, 1863, defined the lay of the land and pinpointed fleet locations, both of which greatly enhanced understanding. To Dana MacBean I offer sincere appreciation.

Louis N. Brown at Beaufort National Cemetery was full of warmth, reverence, and knowledge as he spoke about the cemetery, and it was a pleasure to meet with him. Joel Cadoff with the National Park Service at Fort Pulaski assisted in finding and providing a digital photograph of the 48th New York Volunteers with a baseball game in the background. I am grateful to both men for their help in enriching this book with facts and photo.

From the start Rebecca Kendall has been enthusiastic and helpful in the project, particularly with searches at the New York Public Library and on the web. I am indebted to Rebecca for the research and encouragement she has provided throughout this endeavor. Her support is deeply valued.

Although Joseph's astrological chart and explanation are tangential to the story, they do provide an interesting dimension for those readers inquisitive or curious about astrology and how it may have played out in Joseph's life. I owe much to Beth Guy, who provided the chart of his planetary placements and detailed their associations on the day of his birth.

Without the letters of Joseph, Moses, and Henry, there would be no family history, no book. I am inordinately grateful to Nahum and Lydia, who 150 years ago did not have the heart to let the letters go and to the generations afterward who had the foresight to save them.

FAMILY AND FRIENDS

		Age in 1861
Nahum Manchester	Father	56
Benjamin Manchester	Brother to Nahum	58
Jacob Manchester	Brother to Nahum	62
William Manchester	Brother to Nahum	60
William Manchester Jr.	Cousin to Joseph K.	22
Nahum Manchester	Cousin to Joseph K.	20
Lydia (Austin) Manchester	Mother	55
Moses Austin	Brother to Lydia	41
Benjamin Austin	Brother to Lydia	47
Eben F.	Brother to Joseph K.	29
Maria (Varney) Manchester	Wife of Eben F.	20
Henry W.	Son of Eben and Maria	2
Henry B.	Brother to Joseph K.	26
Rebecca E.	Sister to Joseph K.	24
Mary G. (Chaffin)	Sister to Joseph K.	22
Orin Chaffin	Husband of Mary G.	24
Frank Eugene Chaffin	Son of Mary and Orin	2
Joseph K. Manchester	Civil War Soldier	19
Emily J.	Sister to Joseph K.	15
Alice A.	Sister to Joseph K.	13
Seward M.	Brother to Joseph K.	10
Royal B. Manchester	2nd cousin to Joseph	20
Albert W. Manchester	2nd cousin to Joseph	18
Almond Freeman	Brother to Sargent	20

FAMILY AND FRIENDS *continued*

Age in 1861

The 9th Maine, Company K "Windham boys"

George Nason	17
Sargent S. Freeman	23
Elbridge Libby	27
Stephen Libby	19
Amos H. Hanson	25
Albert Graffam	19
Warren Howe	26
Frank Morton	18
Charles E. Morton	24
Estes Strout	21
Nathan A. Strout	25
James L. Small	33

Joseph's friend from the 5th Maine, Company A Windham

Almon Shaw	17

INTRODUCTION

Hidden under the eaves of the farmhouse attic in Windham lay a story in letters, unread for almost 150 years. Their envelopes were nibbled, their ink faded, their edges frayed. They came from places like Washington Territory, Iowa, Florida, and South Carolina. Addressed to Nahum, Lydia, and others in their family, the cherished letters told of experiences and events from distant family members. Among them were thirty-seven letters written home between September 20, 1861, and July 7, 1863, by Nahum and Lydia's Civil War soldier/son Joseph K. Manchester. Also were several from Lydia's brother Moses, who served with Joseph in the 9th Maine Regiment, Company K. Their letters reached across the distance that separated battle from home fronts, and undoubtedly brought comfort to both the writer and the recipient. This book is not intended to articulate an account of the Civil War, however. Instead, its currency is to reveal the Civil War as Joseph understood and experienced it, to come to know Joseph Manchester through his words, and to let those words give him life.

Joseph's original words, rather than their paraphrase, his sometimes unique spelling, his often understated, sometimes broad humor, and his homespun phrasing and sentence style all mirror Joseph as he cast himself through the pages of his letters. Joseph writes of the ordinary and the important. He can be patient, content, and easy to please, or indignant. He has a clear and critical view of right and wrong. He pens with sarcasm and with flair. He is a natural storyteller. Because Joseph enjoyed reading and learning, his grammar and spelling, nonstandard and sometimes imperfect, are reasonably proficient. Similarly, insertions and corrections on his originals lend evidence that, before posting, he would read over his work.

The narratives of his letters provide continuous threads from one instance or event to another and let Joseph tell his own story. For my part, the commentary framing his letters or providing historical background about the wartime activities around him is intended to assist the reader in seeing patterns, connecting story lines, and better comprehending some of the details in his letters.

I have attempted to make the letters more readable by employing a few contemporary edits: inserting punctuation and apostrophes, which were largely omitted, and providing consistency in the use of capitalization. If their meaning is clear, abbreviations were untouched.

This journey to learn about Joseph began with just a few of his letters almost twenty years ago. It took a dramatic turn in 2012 with the uncovering of more letters and the unexpected awareness that, despite the stone that bears his name in Arlington Cemetery in Windham, Maine, Joseph is not buried there. Joseph's grave is in Beaufort National Cemetery, South Carolina, and it is there where the journey's next phase began.

—Carol Manchester
July 2013

Northern Son in the South
1861-1863

Chapter 1

YOUTH

Gershom Manchester lived at the foot of Dutton Hill in Windham's second division on land his father, Stephen, had deeded him. Stephen lived on the "steep and rugged"[1] hill above, in the house he had built in the 1780s, having moved from the original settled division of New Marblehead following his return from Revolutionary War service. When the fourth and final division of Windham became available in 1804, however, Gershom looked to own a parcel and in the first decade of the 19th century had Stephen's house, which he now owned, skidded down the hill and hauled westerly by oxen to the site in North Windham, where it remained until 1994. It is likely that in this house Gershom and Anne delivered four more children to their already large family of nine, and Nahum was the first of the next four to increase it. In January of 1831 Nahum married Lydia Austin and in August of that same year Gershom sold the farm, barn, and acreage to Nahum.

On a wintery March 15, 1842, in the same house that his great-grandfather Stephen Manchester had built and his grandfather had moved, Joseph K. Manchester was born to Nahum and Lydia. He was the fifth child, third son, welcomed as another of the many hardworking hands the poor, rural family would need to carve out a living on the sandy field behind the farm. It is reasonable to imagine that Gershom, who died in 1853 at 91, shared the family legends with Joseph and his siblings as they were growing up: of Stephen's leaving Tiverton, Rhode Island, to follow his first love to New Marblehead (later renamed Windham) and becoming the fourth settler, or of his bravery in defense of the fort and the community. Surely he mentioned Stephen's love of freedom, the hardship at Valley Forge, and the patriotism of Stephen's son Thomas, who died at Fort Ticonderoga. Likely, Gershom spoke of his own Revolutionary War experience and how Maine later entered the union on March 15, 1820, as a *free* state through passage of the Missouri Compromise. So it was only natural that as the slavery issue grew more contentious and congressmen continued to argue heatedly about expansion, recognizing slaves as property, and the right of states to govern themselves, Joseph would take a resolute stand for individual freedom and perpetual unity of the country.

In 1857 the Supreme Court ruled unconstitutional the provision in the Missouri Compromise to prohibit slavery in the Louisiana Territory north of the 36° 30′ latitude line. In private homes and in the halls of Southern state legislatures was talk of secession. In the congressional halls of Washington loomed the imminent potential for war. Christmas 1860 would be the last Christmas holiday that Joseph, and for that matter President-elect Abraham Lincoln, would spend in their respective family homes, for on December 26, 1860, South Carolina filed secession papers and by September 1861, Joseph and "the Windham boys" would be marching to the camp and field rhythms of the snare.

Despite President Lincoln's urgent call for troops in summer of 1861, Joseph's father Nahum, now fifty-six years old, was reluctant to have his son enlist,[2] predominantly for economic reasons. Joseph's brother Eben was a family man, living in a house down the road and not very much available to assist his father. Henry had relocated to the West, where he was carving out a living in Port Madison, Washington Territory. While older sister Rebecca still lived at home, Mary had married Orin Chaffin and now had a son of her own. The Chaffins lived up the road on the other side of the farm property. Also at home were younger siblings Emily, Alice, and Seward, fifteen, thirteen, and ten years respectively. Tall at six feet, nineteen-year-old Joseph was the only male with strong hands and back who could be of significant help to his father.

Two generations later, Lawrence Manchester (1918–1985) would tell of his boyhood chores, which included brushing back the edges of fields; cutting down the fast-growing gray birches; haying off Indian Hill; harvesting, storing, and selling ice; digging muck out from the bogs to spread on and enrich the gardens; growing vegetables; threshing beans; and feeding and tending the horses, cows, chickens, and other farm animals. Very likely several of these were the same chores required of Joseph to help maintain the family. Through letters, deeds, and other documents[3] it is known that Joseph had planned to keep sheep, that Nahum sold lumber, and that there were two mortgages on the farm between 1857 and 1867. Debt was an ever-present resident. It is not surprising, then, that Nahum did not wish to see his son leave the farm for war.

Nonetheless, Joseph urged his sense of duty, patriotism, and belief in the Union cause to his father, who consented finally, upon condition that Joseph send home his pay.[4]

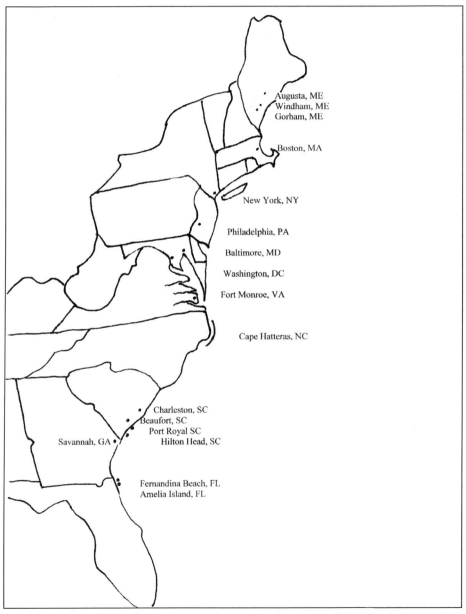

Joseph's travels from Maine to the coastal campaign in the South

Chapter 2

ENLISTMENT

In his September 20 letter home, Joseph reveals his easygoing, upbeat, positive nature, in addition to valuable details and news of the day at Augusta, where the 9th Maine Regiment is being organized.

Father and Mother, Having a few leisure moments I thought I would write and let you know where we are and how we are quartered. We arrived here all safe and sound. We are better situated here than when we were at Gorham. There is 11 companies on the ground now, 1 [one] more than they want to fill the Regt. Uncle Moses Austin is here. He came in one of the Portland companies. He has enlisted in our company. With 8 more that came with him we are nearly full. We got our Uniform last night and it sits nice. We expect to leave here next Thursday. There was a company came about 2 hours after we got here. There was 2 companies arrived yesterday, 1 from Bangor and 1 from Portland. This Company is the first Company now full. It is now called Company A but whether it will be changed or not we don't know yet. I like [it] first rate. We have 2 shirts, 2 pr stockings, 1 pr drawers, 1 pr pants, knapsack, haversack, Cartridge box, Belt, can'teen, blanket, undercoat, overcoat, and cap to each man. We have plenty to eat and that is good enough for anybody to eat. Our pay we expect to get next Monday. We shall be to Portland Thursday if nothing happens. I don't know whether we can get away to come home or not. If I can I shall. We are treated first rate. We have got good officers. Capt. Harding is an excellent officer. He has a kind word for all. We like him first rate. We have had the man at arms this morning. I have not got any time to write any more. I have had to hurry and have not written it very well. Good bye, J K Manchester

Uncle Moses Austin is his mother's brother, about forty-one years old, and throughout Joseph's twenty-two months' service, he and Joseph look after each other and share a friendship and mutual regard beyond the close familial relationship. The phrase "first rate" is one of Joseph's favorites. The next day Joseph tells of a tragedy that had occurred on the 20th.

> *I thought I would write a few lines to let you know the news. There was an accident happened to one of our company yesterday. A party of men went in swimming yesterday and a man by the name of Owen got drowned. He was swimming across the river opposite the camping ground when the cramp took him. Elbridge Libby got to him and got hold of him as he sank the 3rd time. Elbridge sank 2 times with him and got so strangled himself that he was obliged to let go of him or drown. He was in about 20 minutes before he was got out but they could not bring him to. He belonged to L Buxton and leaves a wife and 4 small children. The company is all a going to give his wife $1.00 a piece which will make $100.00 and I expect that most all of the companies will give something. They will get about $200.00 in the whole Regt. I can't write any more at present. J K Manchester to Mrs L D Manchester, No Windham Me*

In the same letter, another message specific to his mother Lydia: *I shall keep my shirt to wear as an under shirt. I almost forgot to say this. The officers have changed the letter of this company. It is K, second in command of the left of the Regt. There is a Bangor company that was here when the 8th left and they claim letter A, or the right of the Regiment. I shall keep my stockings and pants in case I want them.*

Chapter 3

WASHINGTON, DC

And so on September 22, 1861, Joseph was officially mustered into the 9th Maine Regiment Infantry, Company K. Instead of leaving on Thursday the 26th as Joseph anticipated, his regiment was *in* Washington, DC, on the 26th, establishing camp at Bladensburg as part of the capital's defense.[1] They had traveled by steamship and by train.

We arrived at Washington at 11 o'clock P.M. the 25th We staid in Washington the 26th most of the day. We left W about 4 yesterday. We are a mile and a half from the city. It is a handsome place where we are. There is about 60,000 men around and about Washington. There is a rebel encampment 5 miles from here, none any nearer that we know of. We lost one man between Philadelphia and Baltimore. He was on the top of the rear car loading his revolver. The engine gave a sudden jerk and he fell off, we did not know it for some time. After, they stopt the train about 8 miles from where he fell off and went back after him. He was dead when they found him. We fetched the body to Baltimore and left it to be sent home. The 7th Regt is stationed at B. I saw Albert Mathews at B and Geo Bodge and several more that I knowed. The 5th is 8 miles from W. Most of the Me Regts is around W. We are all well here except Elbridge. He had the cramp colic and was carried to the hospital yesterday. He was better this morning. There was 2 of the Regt taken sick at N.Y. by eating pies bought of an old niger. It was thought there was poisen in them. They drove him from the steamer and he had to stay away. We had no more trouble anywhere. The people at Baltimore had union flags in their hands and on the houses. There was more soldiers than you could shake a stick at. The seceshionsts there dare not say one word about seseshion. If they do they will catch it I tell you. We ate dinner on Boston Common and eat supper in Philadelphia. Some ways apart the meals was. I tell you there is no news of importance here now. There is no danger of the rebels attacking Washington. There is too many men there for that. I can look out of the door of the tent in which I am writing and see more than 2,000 men paraded before their camps about ½ mile from the capitol. [The capitol] is in full sight of the rebels. From here it sets on a hill. It is a very large building. It is more than 200 feet from the ground to the observatory top. Uncle Moses and Uncle Benjamin is here, well and hearty and contented. Tell Wm Stevens he acted honorably, very honorably. He is respected, spocken very highly of in the company; but never mind, all of that sort is out of the company. [Joseph writes the sentence about William Stevens with sarcasm; the cause will come to light soon in letters to follow.] *There is a good set of fellows. Now we passed Chestnuts any quantity of them between Philadelphia and Baltimore and stopt under one tree and knocked some but it was hard work to get them out of the burr. You can't pick one of them up no more than you can a thistle head. They are not quite ripe yet. Tell Seward I think I shall be at home in 3 months. I think this trouble will be settled in that time. You must not be worried about me for I am well and doing well. Did you get the Clothes I sent home? You must Direct your letters to J K Manchester 9th Maine Regiment Company K Maine volunteers or MV Washington Dist Columbia. M V is just as good as the whole name. Write as soon as you get this and let me know how things stand at home. Tell A Freeman* [that] *Sargent is well. He is Corporal and he makes a first rate one too...*

This September 27 letter describing the Union regiments in the surrounding area and the proximity of Confederate troops to Washington illustrates the government's very real concern in the summer of 1861 that Confederate troops might march on the capital. But it also reveals Joseph's confidence in the strength of Union troop numbers and his optimism that the conflict soon might be settled so that he could be home in three months. His stories of regimental life, friends, incidents, losses, and events, his homespun description of the Capitol building from the flap of his tent, and his natural use of metaphor to describe a chestnut burr likewise characterize a smart young man with a keen interest in the happenings around him. The Uncle Benjamin Joseph mentions is also a brother to his mother and to Moses Austin, and Seward is his ten-year-old brother back home in Windham. A(lmon) Freeman is Joseph's age, a brother to Sargent, and very likely a boyhood friend from Windham, since Joseph mentions him periodically in letters that follow.

As with most soldiers far from home, a recurrent theme is the request for letters. In this next letter, with tongue-in-cheek chastisement, and in most of his subsequent letters, Joseph urges his parents to send letters. Also, watches are an important item, for Joseph first refers to one here and in later letters writes of his own. Moses and Nahum also will write about his watch.

Chapter 4

ANNAPOLIS

Anapolis Oct 11th 1861

Father and Mother,... I should like to hear from home. I have wrote to you twice and have not received any answer yet. I wrote a letter Sept 27th and 2 since that and I have not received any answer from either of them. I should [like] to know if I have got any friends to home … we are encamped about ¾ of a mile from the city of Anapolis. I have not been in the city yet so I can't tell you any thing about it. There was a fellow Drumed out of the Regt today. He was a kind of a sucker to the Regiment. He said his name was McClellan, a cousin to Gen McClellan, but I guess not. He took a watch from a fellow. At least it was laid to him. The watch belonged to one of the Company C's boys. We have got two new cooks, Uncle Moses and a man by the name of Giles. We have plenty to eat and drink since they commenced to cook. I work with them in the Cooking Camp. The men are all well that came from Windham except Elbridge S Libby has been sick ever since we got here. I don't know what ails him. We are going to move from here tomorrow. The Col says we are going to Wilmington NC. We can get any quantity of nuts here. There is Chestnuts, Walnuts, Peacan nuts, Persimmons, and more kinds than I can think of. I would bet you would laugh if you could see the teams out here. There is hardly any horses here, mules mostly. The driver has a saddle on the near mule and drives with one rein reaching to the near forward one and across to the [ring] of [the other] one's bit. It is fun to see them drive. I tell you you can not understand there talk they have over to there mules. General Scott says we shall eat our Christmas dinner at home. I don't think so. I want you and mother to write as soon as you get this and write all the news.

Sharing impressions of the teams and their drivers adds to the humor of this letter, but the letter also reveals his growing doubt about a quick end to the conflict and returning home for Christmas, despite General Winfield Scott's optimism. Although Elbridge survives his illness, Joseph's mentioning it foreshadows the fact that during the course of the war sickness and disease would take more lives of soldiers than would fatalities from actual combat.

Evidently letters from home arrived for Joseph later that day, as he had a lot to tell in his return letters on October 12th. First, to his father:

> *Dear Father, It is with much pleasure to seat myself to answer your letter I received yesterday dated Oct 6th You spoke of my being contented. I never was better contented in any place in my life. We are comfortably situated about 2/4 of a mile from the city of Anapolis. We live first rate, have plenty to eat and drink, we have Coffee all of the time. We have Beef and potatoes, Sugar and Rice, Molasses, Salt and Beans a plenty. If that is not good enough for anybody I should like to know what is. You spoke also about my Clothes. I will now tell you about them. I have got 1 pair of pants, 2 pair of drawers, 1 pair of shirts, 2 pair of stockings, 1 under coat, 1 over coat, 1 pair of shoes, 2 Blankets 1 of Rubber and 1 of Wool, 1 Bed Cap and towel. Everything I want I have got. I kept my hat and old pants and my Cotton shirt to wear as an under shirt. We hire our shirts and things washed and have to pay 4 cents an article for washing and ironing, cheap enough I think. We expect to move from here soon to go to Wilmington, North Carolina. We expect to winter there. There has been some talk about our going to Texas but that has blown over. I want all of my friends at home to write to me that can write all of the news. I was sorry to here that Aunt Anna was dead. If William was out here he would feel better, I think, than he does now. If I never get back but by running away I never shall come. There has been fun enough about Bill's running away from the company, but they don't say anything about it now. Tell Albert and Royal and Almond Freeman to write to me … tell Seward to keep the belt I sent him to remember me by. I shall be home one of the days, so*

good by from your son, J K Manchester to Nahum Manchester. Write as soon as you get this. [And in 1 inch high letters for emphasis:] *Write often, JKM to NM*

To Seward: *you see Albert and tell him to write to me. Tell him I will answer his letter and be sure to tell him now. Good by, Seward J K Manchester*

Remarkably, although Nahum's letter is written on the 6th, Joseph writes back on the 12th. Montgomery Blair, postmaster general during Lincoln's administration, had transformed a primitive postal system to an efficient service that included military-based postmasters and stamp agents. While Joseph preferred to provide his own postage for the most part, among his letters are several envelopes stamped "postage due 3 cents." Blair's innovative system permitted soldiers to send mail without postage as long as the recipient was willing to pay the postage at his or her end. Moreover, mail, newspapers, and packages from and to home were imperative to morale, and, consequently, tremendous efforts were made to get the mail through despite foul weather and muddy roads.

To his mother:

Was very glad to hear from home and to hear how well father was getting along with his fall's work. We have been here about 4 days. We don't know how long we shall stay at this place. You mentioned Wm Stevens. You said something about his pass. He run away from Augusta the day we was mustered into the service. He did not get any pays or furlough. He run away with about half a dosen more of the same stamp. I shall get an honerable discharge or else I shall stay till the war is ended before I come home. This very minute that I am writing there is a regiment going by up the road farther to join us in the same brigade ... soon to be one great battle that will decide the conquest between the North and South and when that is fought I think it will be settled and we shall then return home again unless we are wanted to keep the Southerners in check. There is so many troops about Washington that it takes 75,000 loaves of bread to feed the soldiers a day besides the other food they eat. 1 man cannot eat one of the loaves of bread a day ... another regt a going past so I must go out to see them. I will finish it when I come in. I will finish this letter now. There has been 2 regts passed within 15 minutes. The first was the 7ᵗʰ Connecticut; the last one is the 50ᵗʰ Penn. There is a terrible powerfull Army out here. You cannot go or look any way but you see Regiments of union troops. The country is full of men ...

General George B. McClellan had been building up the Army of the Potomac in preparation for an eventual advance into Virginia; his troop buildup may be that to which Joseph alludes. The battle at Ball's Bluff and troop movement around Leesburg, Virginia, would occur on October 21.

To his sister Rebecca, he shares his observations of the cities through which he has passed on his way to Annapolis:

I am glad you thought of me away from home. I am well and contented for it is no use to be otherwise. I was much disappointed in the places we passed. New York looked poor and filthy to me. I don't know how it looked to the rest of the men. Boston Common was the prettiest place I have seen yet. Philadelphia I could not tell how it looked. We passed through in the night.

Greatly impressed with the size of a building, he adds, *we ate supper in a place where the folks said they had gave a meal to 40 Regiments. The room was as long as from our house to Uncle Jacobs I should think. I never saw so long a room I think, before in my life.* An early, undated map of Windham shows Jacob's house about 900 feet north of the family farm and across the road.

To Emily, Alice, and Seward:

Dear sister Emily, I will write a line to you with the rest. I have not much to write as I have written all I can think of to father and mother. Be a good girl and write as often as you can. There is so many of you at home, if I should write to all it would take all of my time.... Alice you too be a good girl and write as soon as you can. Seward, be a good boy. Help father all you can. When I get home you shall have a present if I live. Good by all as one.

Evidenced by messages to his father, "*If I never get back but by running away I never shall come,*" and to his mother, "*I shall get an honerable discharge or else I shall stay till the war is ended before I come home,*" it is clear that Joseph is a man of honor and duty. Embedded in his note to Seward is his concern for their father and the possibility that Joseph may not survive the war.

Chapter 5

COATZACOALCOS

Within a few days of the fall of Fort Sumter in April 1861, Lincoln proclaimed a blockade of all Southern ports.[1] Derisively dubbed the "Anaconda Strategy" by the press and political opponents of the administration,[2] intent of the blockade was to put an economic stranglehold on the South by preventing trade with Europe and others through its ports. Over the summer it became obvious, however, that the Confederate ports of Charleston, South Carolina, and Savannah, Georgia, were thriving bases of operations and safe havens for blockade runners, and that Union control of these ports was vital to a successful blocking strategy that initially operated out of Hampton Roads, Virginia, and Key West, Florida.[3] Having safe harbor refuges, coaling stations, and maintenance facilities for the ships, in addition to locations for headquarters and provisioning, would be imperative if the Union's naval command and its infantry were to interrupt trade operations in these ports. And so a joint Army-Navy operation was planned, Port Royal, South Carolina, having been selected ultimately for its deep channel and two-mile-wide harbor entrance. Further, it was more or less midway between Charleston and Savannah. On October 29, Captain Samuel F. DuPont set sail from Hampton Roads for Port Royal with a convoy of more than sixty-five vessels — warships, coal and supply ships, troop transports — and as much secrecy as possible![4] Joseph's next letter is dated October 26 and written aboard the United States mail steamer *Coatzacoalcos*, off Fortress Monroe.

> *Father and Mother, I will now try and answer your letter I received some time ago. I should have answered your letter before but I could not for we were on the vessel and could not get it*

ashore. We came on board last Monday [the 21st] *and sailed for this fort* [which is positioned between Hampton and Norfolk, Virginia]. *We got here Tuesday night and have been here ever since. We are under sealed orders. We don't know where we are going to. We landed on the fort yesterday and went around the outside. We did not go in to it. It is situated in a pleasant place.*[5] *There is 200 guns on this fort mounted, besides one large one they call the Union gun. It is the largest gun that is in the service. It takes 52 lbs of powder to load it. The ball weighs 416 lbs. It is big enough for a man to sleep in comfortable. There was a sloop and a brig brought in yesterday that was captured from the rebels. The brig was loaded with sugar, molasses, and other things. It was quite a prise. Sargent Freeman is sick. They are going to send him home. I think they have just carried him away from here.* [Sargent Freeman would die from his illness five days later, November 1.[6]] *Elbridge is sick yet. I don't know what they are going to do with him.* [Elbridge, however, recovers and survives the war.] *You spoke of my money. I shall send it home as fast as I get it. I should like to see you all but I can't so I must be contented with writing and want you, father, to buy the sheep we talked of and keep them just as you and I agreed on. If I never get home do with them as you see fit ...*

To his mother he sends assurances and writes of gifts for his younger siblings. *I have got good clothes to wear and a plenty of them.... We have had plenty to eat so far. I am going to send Seward and Alice some shells I dug in sand yesterday and want them to keep them.*

Tell little Franky I want to see him and little Henry W too. [The boys are Mary's and Eben's children, respectively.] *Tell all the folks and friends that I know to write to me for I look for a letter every mail. There is so many at home to write to that I can't write to every one at once and shall answer them as fast as I can. Tell Eben and Maria I shan't write to them till they write to me. I was very glad to have a letter from Albert. I can tell who my friends are at home and how much they think of me when I am away and know it is a good ways from here home, but a letter can come in 4 days from home.*

In acknowledging those who sent him letters and chiding those who hadn't, Joseph, it seems, especially misses his family and home this day.

Thoughts of home echo further in his note to Mary: *I received yours and was glad to hear from you.... I should have answered this letter before but we embarked on board the U.S. mail steamer Coatzacoalcos and that prevented me from answering the letter before. Tell little Frank not to forget his Uncle. I won't him. I think of him often. I should like to have him here with me to sleep with me in my berth. Write as soon as you get this. Tell Orin to write to me. Tell Mister Shaw's folks we have had a letter from Almond. He is well. As usual tell Almond Freeman I don't think much of him. He might write to me I should think.... Write as soon as you get this. Oh, I liked to have forgot. Send me some* [news] *papers. From your Brother, JK Manchester to Mary G. Chaffin*

Finally, Joseph receives a letter from the very infrequent writer, his sister Rebecca, and one from Emily. He sends a few lines in return to each of them. Obvious in his responses is his joy in hearing from them. Especially revealing is his paramount honesty regarding the desertion of William Stevens. Not only is he interested in the local happenings at home, requesting newspapers from each of his sisters, but also he offers to send some papers when he can get them so that his family can stay relatively current on perspectives in the South as well.

Still aboard the *Coatzacoalcos*, Joseph writes home on October 29, 1861, the same day that Capt. Samuel F. DuPont and his armada left Hampton Roads, Virginia.

> *Dear Sister, It is with a feeling of gratefulness that I set myself or rather lay in my berth to answer the letters I received from you and Emily. I did feel very sad when I read Emily's letter and am very sorry for Mr. Stevens. It is a great misfortune to lose an arm or any limb but I can't say that I feel so bad for him as I should. If he had got an honorable discharge from the army he might have been here alive & well for aught I know to the contrary. He deserted the company, ran away from Augusta the day we mustered into the service, and traveled all the way from there to Portland on foot. It don't look very likely to me that they if they had got a furlough they would have taken there uniform off & started on foot. I have got so far and am alive and well.*

If nothing happens I shall go further south. I don't want you to worry about my suffering for under clothes. I have got a pair of stockings and a pair of drawers that I have not had on at all. I shant suffer for anything for 2 months to come. We are allowed 3 dollars a month for clothing. It don't cost us half of it. I spilled my ink yesterday and have got to write with a pencil now till I can buy some more ink. There is no news of importance. I got your letter yesterday after I wrote. We are laying here at anchor off Fortress Monroe. We expect to start from here soon. We don't know where we are going to yet. You must write often as you can and write all of the news. I want you to send me some [news] papers, I don't care what kind, some transcripts if you can get them. I must write Emily, so good by Rebecca, from your brother, Joseph K. Manchester

Dear Sister Emily, I received your letter with pleasure. I was very sorry to hear of William's misfortune.... He has got a great deal to suffer.... He might perhaps have got home alive & well from the war and if not he could have had it much worse. At any rate I should rather have heard he was killed outright than mangled up in that way. I should send you some papers if I could get them. Tell Rebecca I forgot to mention Sargent. He was carried away yesterday. They are going to send him home if he don't get better soon. Tell Albert to write to me whether he hears from me or not. [He nears the end of his letter with a bit of humorous sarcasm regarding his friend Almond, and then continues to urge others to write.] *Tell Almond Freeman to write to me. I will answer his letter if he will … write me good long letters. I have got time enough to read them. Write to Mary and Orin and tell them to write to me. Tell Eben he can do as he is a mind to about writing to me. Tell father to buy the sheep as he and I talked of and keep them the same. I can't think of any more to write at present so I must close by bidding you good by from your Brother J K Manchester to Emily J. Manchester. Direct your letters to the 9ᵗʰ Me Regiment Co K, 2ⁿᵈ Brigade, Shirmans Division, to the care of Col D. D. Tomkin, New York, NY. Write as soon as you get this.*

Joseph asks that his mail now be directed by way of Shirmans (Sherman's) Division. General Thomas W. Sherman was to organize a twelve-thousand-man infantry force, Sherman's South Carolina Expeditionary Corps, that would take and hold the harbor's points of land in Port Royal Sound once its protecting forts had been reduced by naval gunfire from Capt. Du Pont's war ships.[7] Joseph's 9th Maine Regiment was a unit of that infantry force. Surely, when he was writing them, Joseph little realized the historical significance and value of his detailed letters to subsequent generations a century and a half later.

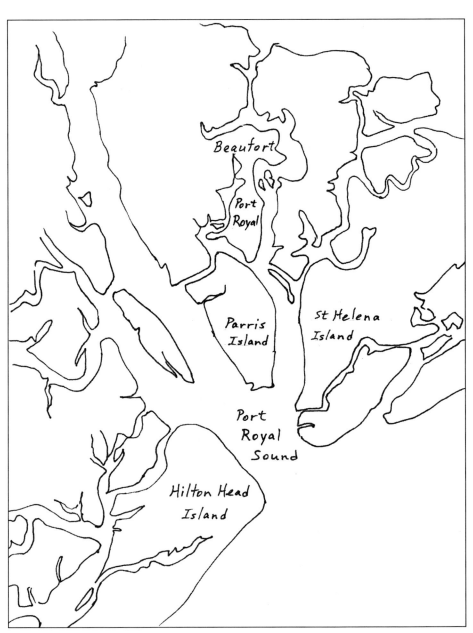

The Sea Islands around Port Royal Sound, about sixty miles from Charleston harbor

Chapter 6

PORT ROYAL *and the* SEA ISLANDS

Joseph's next letter is written from Port Royal, South Carolina, November 13, 1861. During the interval between this one and his earlier letter, much had transpired. The journey south was not an easy one for Du Pont's fleet, nor for Joseph's ship. On November 1 a hurricane-strength storm off Cape Hatteras scattered the Union commander's ships. Moreover, the Confederate Secretary of War Judah Benjamin sent word to South Carolina Governor Francis Pickens and General Thomas Drayton that an enemy fleet was headed for Port Royal. The secret was out.[1] Lieutenant Aaron H. Chase, writing in 1895 of the "History of the 9th Maine Volunteer Infantry, Company H," mentions that "The boat [*Coatzacoalcos*] that the 9th Maine was on had four feet of water in the hold. The men worked the engines for three hours with bars, assisting the engine at every revolution by using iron bars on the walking-beam. The captain of the boat called for volunteers from the soldiers to help work the boat. Thirty men came to his help, and these, he said after the storm, saved the boat. The thirty were all seamen."[2]

About the storm Joseph simply writes: *We liked to have been lost in the gulf stream. We had quite a time but we escaped alive and well, all of the regiment.* Data from the National Hurricane Center indicate that the fiercest day of the storm was November 2, with winds reaching around 80 miles per hour.[3]

The battle for Port Royal, one of the wealthiest, cotton growing "Sea Islands," took place November 3–7, 1861, in Port Royal Sound, a wide expanse of water between two forts. It was one of the more easily gained Union victories, in part because forts on either side of the sound were outmanned and outgunned, and with careful maneuvering Union ships could evade much of their cannon fire. This is not to say that the

Union went without damage or fatalities.

In late afternoon on the 7th, the twelve-thousand-man landing party went ashore, following a naval battle that had lasted throughout most of the day and had effectively cleared the way for union occupation.[4] From his letter of November 13, Joseph's perspective follows:

> *The rebels had quite a stronghold here but we took it without much trouble. We lost on board of the ship 12 killed and a number wounded. The rebels' loss must have been great. We found in the fort 20 dead bodies and down by the woods we found where they had buried a number more. The negrows say the rebels carried carts full of their dead and wounded off to the main land. They run just like a flock of sheep with a dog after them. We are bound to give it to them where ever we can meet them. We have got quite a number of rebel prisoners that could not get off the island in time to escape us. They left about 80 Cannons, some small arms, provisions, and other stuff. The guns were English pieces showing that they have traded with England to get them.*

The "negrows" Joseph mentions are those slaves left behind when the wealthy plantation owners fled to the mainland. Prior to the conflict, it was practice for landowners to leave slaves on the Sea Islands under the supervision of a trusted overseer while the owners remained in the cooler comfort of their mansions on the mainland; and so leaving their slaves behind is not surprising. His letter also confirms the government's fear that England is supplying materials and munitions to the Confederacy.

Showing optimism and his ever-present humor, he continues: *We have got 3 of the rebels' gunboats at anchor off the fort. There was one steamer loaded with the inhabitants of Beaufort come down to see the fort sink the Yankees as they call us but their specks fell some ways below their noses. If we carry things along at this rate we shall be at home in the spring, at least I hope it will be settled by that time.*

Earlier in this letter he had written, *I am going to send you some cotton I picked out here in the field. It looks curious to see it growing with the pods, the blows* [bolls], *and the ripe cotton on the same stalk. I want to send some seeds if I can in this letter but they are so big I don't expect I can do it.* Intrigued by this southern phenomenon of cotton, Joseph wished to send a simple gift to Emily. Very likely it was the region's well-known Sea-Island cotton, greatly valued for its long, silky fibers.

On the same stationery, Joseph writes to his father. His rhythmic sentence style shows command of the language just as his easy use of comparisons shows rich homespun way of speaking. Other sentences indicate the firm belief that victory is on the side of the North.

> *Dear father,... We are here at Port Royal well quartered, well provisioned, and well clothed so far. It is about as warm here as August. The nights are cool. There is a dew falls here enough to wet the trees so that it will drop off like a shower. We did not have much trouble to take this place considering how strong it was fortified. There is batteries on one side and the fort on the other. The fort had between 50 and 60 cannon. The batteries had 16. There is some batteries on the lower side of the island with 8 cannon but they did [not] have any good gunners or they might have sunk every ship in the bay.*
>
> *I want you to write to me when you have got them sheep for me yet. Get them if you can. I am going to send some money as soon as we get paid.... We expect to be paid of next Monday but we are not certain of it yet.*

Referring, undoubtedly, to the November storm at sea, Joseph mentions a rumor going around camp. *There was a story came from Maine that some one wrote we were lost. It is all humbug. I don't want you to worry about me for I think we shall all be at home by May if not before. The south is getting sick of their bargain already. There was a letter picked up written to some of the rebel officers stating if we took this place and the batteries opposite, that the South might as well give up. We have got both places and are going to have more, I guess you would think, if you could hear the cannon they are firing in the direction of Charleston now. And I have seen fort Sumter with the rebel flag floating over it. The stars and stripes are bound to float over it yet. It is on an island in a place to take, but it has got to surrender. I should like to see them have to pull the rebel flag down. If they don't surrender before long the gunboats that is here will try them a tug and see what they can do about it. I want Emily to send me some papers to read. From your son Joseph K Manchester to Nahum Man-*

chester. Write soon as you get this.

By the time Joseph writes this next letter he has been in service about ten weeks. He has experienced battles and seen death in the eyes of slain soldiers. Additionally, several fellow company members have lost their lives to accidents or disease. More frequently, his lines home echo phrases like "if I live." Even so, his bravery, his pride, and his belief in the rightness of the cause are manifest. So is his youthful enthusiasm. Ten weeks have also taught him to be careful about whom to trust; he is cautious about sending home his money in the form of gold. Also, Sargent Freeman's father has been inquiring about his late son's possessions. It was common for personal items or money not to make it back to family members.

> *Hilton Head South Carolina December 12th 1861*
>
> *Dear father,… I thought I would write to you to let you know of my health which is good at present.* [Lieut. Chase writes that after landing, "the wet conditions, exposure and poor food told on the men fearfully. Fevers, colds and bowel complaints were common."[5]] *I received your letter being date Nov 26, and I was very glad to hear from you. I had not received a letter for 2 weeks before I received this. You spoke of my sending money home. We was paid $17.00 last Saturday but mine is Gold money. I dare not send it in a letter. I trust I shall be at home by the first of May if not before, but if I get killed or wounded I have friends that will send my money to you. I think something will be done in congress to settle this affair. If nothing is done there we shall do something, that's sure. If we have got to fight we have made up our minds we will never leave the field till we conquer. They have boasted and bragged enough. If they want to fight they had better try us here and see how they will get out of it. We are all ready to try a shot with them if they like. I think we shant get a shot at the frightened partridges. They have got a little fort at Bluftown, mounted 3 brass guns. If they want guns for Bluftown and every thing else in that vicinity tore to pieces, let them stay a few days longer. We will run two or three of our gun boats up there and see if they will stand fire as well as they stood it here. Tell Seward to be a good boy, do all the work he can to help father,*

and go to school. Obey your teacher, Seward, and learn all you can. I shall have something to make you all a present if nothing happens when I get home. Perhaps I shall never have the privilege of seeing Maine again but I am in my country's cause. It is no disgrace to die in that. I shall continue to do my duty until I am discharged. Uncle Moses and Benjamin is here with me. They are the best friends I have got. The rest are here all well and hearty. The general opinion is that we will be at home by spring if not before. The news is favorable....

Dear Mother, I will write a line or two to you as you think of me most every letter so I will think of you. You wanted me to send you some seseshon [secession] Cotton. I will send some if I can get it in the next letter. There is a whole field of it but I have got to pass the guard to get to it. We go out to work on the fort⁶ every other day. Then I can get enough of it to answer your demand. I am sorry I have not got any to send you this time but you shall have some next letter if I can get it possibly. Tell Mary E. I thank [her] for the paper she sent me. I will try to find something to send her. You spoke of their getting some things for us. If you have any things to send you can direct them to me. I shall get them. Lieut Shaw's Brother is getting some things for us. You had better trust them to him. You said Mr Freeman wanted to know what property Sargent had with him. I don't know what he had. He had a watch and about $50.00 in money as far as I can learn.

About six weeks intervene before this next letter, and during that time Joseph's company has been shipped to Fernandina Beach, Florida, and then back to Hilton Head. His youthful enthusiasm abounds.

Hilton Head Port Royal SC Jan 22ⁿᵈ 1862
We have been removed from Fernandina, and since we left, the rebels have been raising Cain with the Regt we left there. They say they have got the Col, his wife, all the pickets but four that was on at the time, and over one half the Co that guarded the Bridge. The rebels made their brags that if ever the 9ᵗʰ Maine ever left there they would raise the D----l with them. But enough of

this. Uncle Benjamin will tell you all about it, he is coming home. He is here. He has been discharged nearly three weeks and has been waiting for a chance to get home. I expect we shall have to go back to Fernandina again. If we do we may in all probability have to fight to get it again. We can hold it alone if no other Regiment can't. Uncle Benj is going to send me some things that I want out of the money he owes me; therefore he will not pay you the money I told you he would. I have sent you a shaving box by him. Inside of it is a piece of Resin for Royal[6] and some Rebel powder for Albert. We have not been paid of yet. The men complain very much because they don't get their money. For my part I wait the issue of events. It is no use to grumble. I don't know as I have anything more to write. Uncle B will tell you the rest. I forgot to mention that I received a letter from Mother but we had to move which prevented me from answering it. Tell mother I will write to her soon.

    Hilton Head SC Feb 12 1862
    Dear Father,… My health is good at present and hope these few lines will find you the same. I am going to send you 15.00 in this letter, and if it arrives safe I shall send more soon. 15 is as much as I dare send to once … paid of day before yesterday … 6 months' pay. I shall send most of it home as I don't want it here. I shall keep enough this time to last me. I haven't been a very great spendthrift since I have been in the army.

Since Joseph is well aware that limited cash is his father's ever-present situation, he levels edgy criticism at his brother Henry, who is in Washington Territory working for a lumber mill and writing home of the good money one can make there. *I think if Henry had done as much as I have considering his chance to get money, but perhaps he knows his business best. At least he ought to.*

He's not too pleased with his uncle either. *I want to know if Uncle Benj has got home. He went away $4 in debt to me. I don't know as ever I shall get a cent of him again, but if he don't pay me he-d better never see my face again. He hasn't used me just right in a good many things that I could mention. If he does as he agreed to it will be all right between him and me,* *but if he don't I want you to get it from him.*

I want to know if Almond Shaw is killed or not. I have heard that the 5ᵗʰ Maine was most all killed in them late battles. I haven't heard from him … since I have been out here.[8]

Tell Albert I want him to write to me, if he don't I will pull his ears for him when I get home. Tell Maria I should be pleased to hear from her. [He asks that Rebecca and Emily write also and says that he will try to write Mother, Seward, and Alice "by and by."] *Do the best you can until I get home and will try and do the same.* He also inquires after Henry and Eben.

At the end of the letter to his father is this note to his mother; three details are of particular note. Her brother Moses has become lame now. Moses suffered from chronic rheumatism, which would hospitalize him occasionally and plague him the rest of his life. In an infrequent display of overt affection, he writes "good bye <u>dear</u> mother," and he wants to draw her attention to the money he sent. *Dear Mother,… The men are all well with a few exceptions. Uncle Moses is lame yet and I don't doubt if ever gets well again out here. Uncle Ben has got home before this time. He will come up there I expect soon. He promised me he would as soon as he got home. I can't think anymore to write at present so good bye, Dear mother. Take notice what there is wrote in the pieces of paper inside and let me know, will you please? J K M L D Manchester*

Sometime around January 1862, in a letter to their son Henry, Nahum and Lydia must have asked if he could come home in the spring. Henry wrote back on February 9, 1862. *"I cannot give you a definite answer about coming home, you know. I come out here to make a little something and I have to come home, leave good wage here and have to go to work for 14 or 15 dollars per month. If I come home now I shall come back again soon and I know you will not want me to come back, and so I think I had better stay a while longer now I am here."* Earlier in January he had written that he had summer prospects of earning $75 per month.[9]

Elsewhere in his February letter Henry wrote, *"You spoke of selling Charley. When you can, sell anything for what it is worth, allwaise sell it, but you must act your pleasure about that."* He added, *"I sent you a check a short time ago for one hundred dollars $100 and before you get this you will undoubtedly receive it."*

Hilton Head SC March 11ᵗʰ 1862

Dear Mother, I hasten to answer your letter I rec'd to night as the mail goes out tomorrow morn at 6. I must hurry and write, and anything done in a hurry cannot be done well. [Now there's a lesson taught at home!] *The same by this letter (so you will excuse this scribbling it is not writing). I am well as usual, the rest of the boys is well except Albert Graffam. He is lame in the back and hips with the rheumatism ... has been lame some time. I don't know how long. Uncle Moses is writing so there is not need of my writing anything about him. I am glad you got the money I sent home. I was afraid I had lost it. I shall send $20 more soon. I guess I shant send it in this letter. If Rebecca wants a sewing machine Uncle M and I can make out money enough. M to buy it for her. Tell her so. Tell her to write how much it will cost and she shall have the money if I have to borrow it. Try your best and get that money from B ... and use it yourself. I guess I shant need any watch. I thought of it but I guess I shant need any for I might lose it. You had better get the money safe at home than run the risk. You spoke of sending a box of things to me. I will write and let you know when to send that. Tell A. Manchester I haven't got any* [mail] *from him yet. Ask him if he directs his letters right. If he directs them to Fla I shant get them, perhaps that is the reason of it. You spoke of Uncle B boarding out among strangers. (He told us here and kept a regular correspondence with a woman by the name of Abba Hanson.) He told us he was married to her the next day after he enlisted but I don't believe it. If he was married he wouldn't be boarding out. You wanted to know of our movement. We are doing guard, drill, fatigue, police, provost duties, and likely to continue so some time longer. I don't think we will get to Charleston. The talk is we are going to stay here to garrison this island but we don't want to stay. We want to see them skeedad ... from C.* [Charleston]. *It is dull and tiresome here without any excitement at all. We have heard here that US treasury notes such as we are paid of in are not good in Maine. Write if it is true or false.*

And with understated, loving banter, he continues, *you thought you had worried my patience but you have not. Nothing is more acceptable than a good long letter. If I haven't worried your patience this time it can't be worried at all. Excuse all imperfection.*

Then adding a few marks of punctuation (;:........--!), he writes: *put these in where they are needed. Yours hastily, Joseph K Manchester to L D Manchester*

Chapter 7

FERNANDINA

Joseph now is situated in Fernandina, Florida. Confederates had taken over Fort Clinch at the start of the war but Federal troops had regained it on March 3, 1862. The fort and the town of Fernandina Beach now are under Federal control. Companies D & H of the 9th Maine went into Fort Clinch and remained there ten months doing "drill, picket and guard duty."[1] Only officers were quartered inside the fort, however, according to an interpreter at Fort Clinch in October 2012, though it is probable that soldiers living outside the fort frequented the commissary inside the fort. Joseph and his unit lived outside the fort.

March 17, 1862, and still with a sense of humor despite his suffering, Joseph pens a letter home.

> *Dear Father, Having a few leisure minutes I thought I would spend them in letting you know of my health which is not the very best at present. I have got the mumps. They are rather painful but they are not very bad. They make my hand tremble so I guess you will have to get a lawyer to read this for you. But I guess some of you can read it.*

It is well known that more men died from close contact diseases and unsanitary camp conditions than died from wounds during the Civil War. Since many of the soldiers came from distant, isolated areas, camp life in the new locations crowded them together and exposed them to new and contagious illnesses. This fact may explain why Joseph so often began his letters or included references about his health or the health of his uncles and fellow Windham boys. The letter clearly reveals Joseph's continued awareness of his father's financial straits.

We was paid of today four months' pay $52.00. I shall trust $25.00 in this letter for I know your circumstances as well as you do, but if I lose it I shall have $25 dollars more which I shall send by express. I dare not trust any more [than] *this this time. Twenty dollars is enough to lose, if it is my luck to lose it, but I trust will go safe. My hand trembles so bad I can hardly write as you can see by the pot hooks and trammels I make. Give my best respects to all enquiring friends and tell them all to write to me. If this goes safe I will send more. Tell Mr. H.H. Boody I am alive and kicking yet.* [H. H. Boody, affluent businessman and lawyer in town, had been holding a mortgage note against Nahum's farm since August 1858.] *Tell him you have got one friend in the world.*

I can't hold my pen still enough to write much more so good by from your son J K Manchester to Nahum Manchester. I shall have to get my friend Corporal Cooley to back it for me, my hand trembles so bad.

18ᵗʰ—I have received a letter from Henry today. He is well. I am going to write what I am about and if he don't help you I shall do what I can my self alone, but I think if he calculates to come home in the spring he had not better send any. What I can help you to [meaning the money] *I think you can get along* [on]. *J K M*

I forgot to mention Uncle M & B; they are here. Both are well and hearty. I can't write any more for it is as bad as a whipping.

From his letters, it seems that Uncle Benjamin went home and is back in camp again.

In early April Nahum and Lydia receive a letter from Forest Higgins, a friend of Joseph.

You will probably be surprised in receiving a letter from me who is a perfect stranger, but I will make no excuses. Your son Joseph is at present quite sick all month. He is not confined to his bed ... has been with the Doct Hanuk for some time. But we do not think it is anything alarming with good care. We think he will soon get over it as he [is] in the mending hand. The course of this illness is he over heated himself in general. He ... had an attack of the Mump but he's recovered from. You may rest assured he has the best care. This is possible to give one situated as near. He tent[s] with his Uncles Benj and Moses who spare no time or expense to make him comfortable.

P.S. Mr. Benj Austin wishes to know what you will [unreadable] him that Cow for. Please write immediately and he will send you the money and get you to drive the cow home for his gun.

About five weeks later, April 20, 1862, Joseph sends letters to his parents. Significant in these letters is his continued concern for the family's burdensome debt, his generosity and sense of family commitment, and his efforts to bolster Nahum's morale. He offers that with money so tight Nahum need not buy the sheep they had talked of. He is both pleased to hear from and proud of his youngest sibling, Seward.

Dear Father,... I was very glad to know that my money I sent had got home. I shant be able to send the other 25.00 in this letter as it is up to camp and I am in the hospital. I am well and hearty but the doctor won't let me go to the company yet. I have got all well of the mumps. They was very painfull. I am all right now, father. I don't want you to sell the oxen or horse if you can help it. I shall send the other 25 dollars as soon as I get out of this, but we have first rate quarters here. We sleep in a good bed, we have a pretty good time here after all. You need not buy any sheep this winter. Take the money to help yourself with. I want to tell you something [about] the climate and productions. The weather is as warm as it is to home in June, the corn here is knee high with every thing else to match. Father, you must keep up good courage. You must not be down hearted one mite. I will help you all I can. If Henry tried, he might do a great deal for you. When I get the other 25 home it will make 93 dollars I have sent. If Henry had done as well considering his pay as I have he could have had it all settled up before this time. I begin to think he don't care how things goes on at home, at least it looks so to me.

You spoke [of] Uncle Moses and Benjamin. They are here, well, and rugged. Uncle Moses is Carpenter for the regiment. All of the Windham boys is well and hearty. We haven't had no trouble here yet excepting Co I. They sent 7 men out on the main land to guard a woman's property and the rebels surrounded the house, shot one and took the rest prisoners. The next day the regiment went over there but the rebels kept out of range. The rebels were mounted and kept out of the way of the rifles. There was a fellow in Company I deserted and they expect he was to the bottom of that affair. He was mad with the sergt that was there and swore vengeance on him. I can't write much more. I was very much surprised in getting a line from Seward. I did not know he could write. I could read his writing quite fast. I want him to write again. He has done wonders in school this winter.

And in a conversational and compassionate tone he writes to his mother:

Uncle Moses and Benj is here … well and hearty. We are gaining ground as fast as ever troops did, but it will be some time before we can drive them from all of there batteries. We have got a great deal of ground to go over yet to conquer. They won't give up till we drive them into the gulf of Mexico. I suppose we are driving them every day. Mother, I will write about Henrys letter in the next mail. It is up to camp and I can get it today when I go up to camp. I shall write and let you know all about it. You must not worry about me. I am well now; I was pretty sick the other day and I got my friend FR Higgins to write to you and let you know how I was. I had not ought to have done it for I expect it has worried you almost to death, but don't worry any more. I feel first rate now. If our troops continue to win the day as they have done for two months past we shall get home by July if not before. They can't stand it much longer I don't think. Mother, let that money go to help father; let it go freely. I can earn more. Money is nothing to me. I don't care nothing about it. It will do father ten times the good it will me. I shall have some money when I get home, if nothing happens, to help myself with and to help you and father with. I hope it will be the will (of) god that we shall get out of debt and more and stand on our own feet again. I will do my best to get clear of H H Boody. I don't want to ever have anything to do with him ever after this.

Apparently Henry's check hadn't arrived, for in an April 9th letter to his parents, Henry writes, *"You spoke of the draft I sent. It was sent from here over 4 four months ago. There is something rong about it. The man that sent it will be here in a few days and then I can find out all about it. Once before I had some trouble about one but it came out all right."*

Uncle Moses doesn't write much in his letters generally, but his few lines are invaluable for what they do reveal, and for such reason are included in this narrative. This letter to his niece, also written April 20, speaks compellingly of his own personal loneliness.

> *Dear friend Rebecca,*
> *I now rite another line to you. I am well and hope you and all of your folks are well. Rebecca I never have received any letters from you except what you roat in Joseph's letter. I requested you to rite and direct your letter me. I have ben waiting to git a letter from you so to send you my mony Rebecca. Rite and let me know if you got a gold dollar I sent to you. Joseph is gitting smart. We are all doing well.*
> *The rebbels shot one of our men last week and we followed him and kiled him and have not time to rite mutch so I will close. Rebecca, I shal look for a letter from you. Yours in haste, Moses Austin*

In the meantime, following receipt of Higgins' letter, Nahum, like any parent anxious about his son's well-being, must have sent a letter to Capt. C.B. Shaw about Joseph's hospitalization, for among the found letters is correspondence from Capt. Shaw. While his tone is reassuring, the captain does seem somewhat miffed at having received Nahum's letter, and by the time the letters have been exchanged Joseph is back at his post.

Fernandina Florida May 9th 1862

Mr. Manchester, Dear Sir,

Received your note today. I was somewhat surprised to hear, or learn, that such news should go so far from here as Joseph's sickness was very light and probably he was on duty before you wrote that note. I will give you a time account of Joseph's sickness.

He was unwell about (5) five weeks but if he had been at home he would (without doubt) been out every day, still he was sick and unfit for duty and that caused such report to reach you. He is now on duty and likes [looks] very well. Yours respectfully, Capt. C.B. Shaw

Joseph updates Rebecca on April 24, detailing military success, deserters, and discipline.

I came out of the hospital yesterday and I feel first rate now. I don't want you to worry so much about me at home for I am doing well. I think this war will be settled up by spring the way things are going on now. We have news of great victorys in Tennessee and Virginia. [Perhaps he refers to Shiloh and to Yorktown, McClellan's siege campaign.] *We have heard that Fort Pulaski is taken; if it is, Savannah comes next. I have seen Fort Pulaski; it is a hard looking fort but it is taken. There was about 400 rebels in the fort at the time. Uncle Moses helped build the batteries that took the fort.*

Joseph is correct about what he had heard regarding Fort Pulaski. The engineer, Capt. Quincy Gillmore, had "erected 11 artillery batteries containing 36 guns and mortars along the northwest shore of Tybee Island"[2] and these very likely are the batteries to which Joseph alludes. The Confederates, who believed the fort was invincible, in part because of its seven-and-a-half-foot-thick walls, the alligators in the wide, swampy moat, and the major reinforced areas, were somewhat cavalier and unprepared for the onslaught of the experimental long-range rifled cannons. After a thirty-hour bombardment April 10–11, Confederate commander Col. Charles H. Olmstead, fearful that the powder magazine was about to blow up and concerned about the lives of his men, surrendered.[3]

That fellow in Co I that deserted, we have got him. The rebels brought him on board the gunboat Ottawa at St. Augustine to exchange him for one of their men that had deserted from them but the Capt of the gunboat told them he did not exchange deserters nor he would not let them take him away with them. We shall probably have to see him shot. It will be a bad sight but we shall have to witness it. He is a bad fellow. I can't pity him much. He has acted bad ever since he has been in the Regt. I can't think of any more to write at present. I must write to Emily as I promised to, so good by Dear Sister, from your brother J K Manchester to Miss R E Manchester.

The 9th Maine Regiment Infantry would remain in Fernandina, Florida, until January 23, 1863.[4] As Joseph indicates next, it is a pretty comfortable assignment and optimism prevails.

May 21, 1862
Dear Mother,… We are in the city of Fernandina quartered in houses. We have got a first rate chance to live. We can keep clean & neat. We don't have to drill but of little. We don't drill any when it is hot. It is very hot most of the time so we don't have to drill much. I received a letter from you the 18th You spoke of the prospect of peace. I think (though I may be mistaken) [that] we shall be at home by the 4th of July. The rebels are completely whipted out of these states. We have been out after scouting parties of them several times but we can't catch them. They are mounted robbers, nothing more or less. We have got 15 mounted cavalry to range the woods round here. We are going to have 35 more. That will be enough for them I guess. Our Company & Company H went of up the river the other day & dug up a 32 pounder that the niggers said the rebels buried there. It is a nice gun. It was a U.S. piece stolen from the Pensacola navy yard in Fla.

He writes that the Windham boys and Uncles Moses and Benj all are well and wants Emily to send the papers she promised to send.

Tell father I have signed $12 a month to be paid him at the *town treasury. I shall send him $20 more in a letter soon. I wrote to him some time ago I would send 23 dollars. I shant be able to send but twenty for I shant have but the one dollar a month ... (you must excuse bad writing & mistakes for I am in A hurry. I am on guard & have to write between the relief).*

Two days later he writes his mother again, suggesting the possibility that he might be home by July. Once more, he mentions his older brother Henry, questions the $100 Henry claims to have sent, and feels keenly that in light of the heavy debt and hardship, Henry too should be helping the family financially.

Dear Mother, Having leisure time I thought I would answer your welcome letters I received yesterday. They were dated May 9th 62. I was glad father was getting along so well with his spring's work. I should like to be at home to help him but I cannot get there until the war closes which I think is near at hand. I don't think it will be many months before it will be settled. We have taken about everything from them that they have got. I can't see where they have got to flee to. Nearly all of the south is covered with our troops. We have been paid and I signed to father 12 dollars per month which he will get at the town treasury when he calls for it. If he wants more to do his spring work with send word and I can send him $20 more, or as much as I can spare. It won't do to spare myself short for a man is without if he is without money. I wrote to Henry the other day. If he receives the letter I think it will wake him up. I think he has acted rather mean to distress father with his debts and not try and help him at all. He ought to think it was coming hard on him. I did and tried my best to avoid it. If he had sent him 100 dollars he would not have lost it. I want father to use all of that money I sent him if he wants it. I should have felt bad if he had kept that money in the house and sold the oxen or horse rather than let it go. I don't want you to worry about me I never felt better in my life. I must now finish this letter. The mail goes at 3 and it is noon.... J K M to L D M very much in haste.

Three weeks later, June 15—Joseph writes of mail issues, ordinary things, Charley, and newspapers.

> *You wrote me you had sent me some papers. I did not get them. I have got 0 papers since I have been out here. There has been some foul play with our mail. Some of our letters had been down to Ship island.... We had 21 recruits came yesterday. Our company got 12 of them. I enjoy good health now. I have not had any humor this spring. We bathe in the salt water twice a week. We keep clean as possible. We live first rate and have good clothes. We don't get any new, except what we get by mail.... You must not think it strange if you don't receive a letter every week. I would like to have you receive a letter every mail but it is impossible....*
>
> *Monday 16ᵗʰ... it is raining hard now. We have just been to dinner ... hard bread and beef for supper, and breakfast we shall have soft bread.... I want to know how Father gets along with his spring's work. Tell him to keep the oxen and Charley until I get home. If he has to sell anything tell him to sell the oxen.... Tell Emily Alice and Seward that I can't write to them this time. They must be patient. I shall be at home soon, by August I hope.*
>
> *I am very sorry I did not get the papers you sent me. You know how I love to read. The rest of the boys get papers and I can borrow them. You spoke of the Capt's letter. I don't know how he wrote. I don't want to come home if I can help it until the Regt comes. I had rather stay until the Regiment comes home than to be discharged. I want to see the end of this rebellion before I come home. I should like for you to send me some post stamps. We can't get them here. This place was all cleared out by the rebels before we got here. The citizens are coming back one at a time and are claiming protection. They are pretty well conquered I tell you....*

This next missive to his parents on July 15, 1862, explains why the mail had been delayed of late and presents a shift in his expectations, both about a quick end to the conflict and of his hope to be home sometime in the next few months. Asking about Henry Boody, suggesting a hired hand, avoiding the sale of Charley if at all possible, and seeking the "news" all connect to his concern about the farm debt. Eagerly he has been awaiting word from them.

I now try to answer your letter which I received yesterday & glad to get a letter from home. I was sorry to hear father was lame. I hope he will get better soon. I don't see much prospect of my getting home for a year or so, the rebels hang on longer than I thought they would. They have got to be whiped from every crack and corner, I expect, before they will give up. The rebels have got two of Company G & 6 of Company J. I don't know but what they will get the whole regiment by piecemeal they [the men in the regiment] *are so careless. They run round just as though there was no enemy at all. You or mother wrote about my money. I thought it would be the best way to prevent losing it. When you write again let me know how much you have got. There is 12 dollars a month from the 1ˢᵗ of March. Let me know if there is any trouble about the money. I thought I could get along with what I had here. I want you to send me some postage stamps. I don't like to write to anybody & not pay the post. I know it don't make so much difference in the letters I send home but if I want to send a letter to anyone else I like to pay the post. Uncle Benjamin has been very ill. He is better now. He is writing at the same table with me now.... We are outside the lines now in the highest house in the city. This house is the lookout where they watch for vessels when they come in. We had been looking for this mail for four weeks. We expected we had lost it. It started from Hilton Head and got drove back 2 times then they put guns on her* [the ship] *and she got here safe. That nest of rebels has got to be cleaned out and they will be. They can't carry on these games long I tell you. I want you to do the best you can, if you can't get along without hiring a man, hire one as cheap as you can and I will pay him.[5] Don't sell the horse if possible, keep him if nothing more. How does Henry Boody carry himself lately?... Write as soon as you get this and let me know all the news.*

I can't write any more at present so good by from your Son J.K. Manchester to N. & L.D. Manchester

The next letter found in the collection is dated Sept 16, 1862. Benjamin, who is 48, seems to have been ill off and on since early summer.

His condition will grow worse over the next few months. At this juncture, Joseph does not know that his brother Eben had enlisted as a private in the 20th Maine two weeks earlier, on August 29.

> *Dear Father,... I have just came off guard and have not had any chance to write before. ...* [He, Uncle Moses, and all the rest of the Windham boys are well but] *Uncle Benjamin has started for home. He has been sick some time. I gave him 10 dollars to give you when he gets home. I want you to be sure and get it. I sent 3 dollars to Hilton Head to get some stamps with. If he don't get the stamps he will give you that also. Write and let me know how the crops came in this fall and let me know who has enlisted lately. Tell Albert and Royal they had better enlist and come out to this company. They might just as well as not.... I got one* [letter] *from Mary and one from Eben and Maria and one from home. It is the first I have received from Eben at all.*

His October 15 correspondence acknowledges Eben's enlistment, reflects his firm belief in its being the right thing to do, and shows Joseph's patriotism and personal, resolute determination to see the war through. Even so, wistfulness pervades the letter. Newspapers from Maine are still not forthcoming, and Rebecca has actually written to Moses. Having lost confidence in the financial arrangement he had established in February regarding his pay, he has decided to resume the original method of sending money home himself. Subsequent letters will indicate the persistent difficulty of actually receiving his money from the government, however.

> *Dear Mother, ... I am very glad you are getting along so well in my absence. I should like to be glad to be at home with you now but it is impossible. The country's cause needs me here at present and I am here to do my duty as a man ought to do, not to stay at home and act the coward as some I know. Perhaps you can take the hint without my calling any names. It would be as well I suppose. I hear that C C Hunt was rejected at Augusta. I would like to know what it was for. I never knowed there was anything the matter with him. It is to bad, we expected to see him as much as we expected to eat again.... Uncle Moses got a*

letter from Rebecca. He answered it the same day he got it. You wrote me you sent me a paper last week or the week before this letter was wrote. I have not received any paper at all. I should like to know what the reason is that I can't get papers as well as the other fellows. I should like to be at home to help father husk some of these evenings very much. You spoke of my money. I am going to have it paid me here. I don't like the proceedings about this allotment role. The Capt and all the rest of the Company has signed to have their money paid them here. I think it best and then I can send it home as I see fit. Father will get the money up to the first of August and after that I shall send him money as I have before. I haven't had but one letter from Henry since I have been out here; he don't write to me very often. Eben wrote me one little note before he went off; he did not let me know he had enlisted. Maria feels very bad about it. I know by the letter she wrote me. She must cheer up, do the best she can now he has gone. He is only doing his duty, the duty of every man in the north. If I was at home today I would enlist again. It is no use to hang back and wait for others to go and do the fighting for them. If the men had enlisted last spring half the number they have got now would have put a stop to this war. I think it would & may be wrong but I don't think so. I am in hopes to get home by next May. I think it can be settled before that time if they push along after the rebels and don't give them any time to fortify new positions. I will close now as it is most dress parade time. Give my love to all enquiring friends. Good by from your son J K Manchester to L D Manchester

On the same stationery a day later, he razzes his father. Also, as a Maine boy, he perceives the southern rivers running through marshes as a "stream."

Dear Father, I will answer your little letter. I can hardly call it a letter it was so small. I am getting along first rate. I am well and rugged; the climate is healthy here. It is cool now about as cool as it is in Maine in September.... The Windham boys is well except Nathan Strout; he has been ailing for some time. There is no news here at present, everything is quiet. The rebels show themselves now and then but dare not engage us for fear of the Gunboat that lies in the stream. If you can't get along without hiring someone, hire some good man to help you and I will try and pay it if I can. I have stopt my money in the allotment role. I am going to have it paid me here. The Captain thinks it is best and so do I.

To Rebecca   *November 12, 1862*

Dear Sister, It is with pleasure I seat my self to answer your letter I just received. I did not know but what you had all forgotten me for I have not had a letter for some time. I am well at present.... Uncle Moses has just finished writing to you. He got a letter in this mail from you. He is very much pleased to get a letter from home. Uncle B has come back. His papers were not right. He is not well yet. He can't speak plain yet. I don't know as he ever will. He don't have anything to do of any consequence. He is getting better I think. Uncle Moses is going to send you his watch to keep for him ... until he gets home. I am going to describe an affair in which the 9ᵗʰ or part of it took part in. Our troops have been with drawn from Jacksonville and since then it has been discovered the rebels were building batteries on a high bluff to keep our boats from going up there. They sent a steamer for 5 companies of the ninth Maine to go and help take it. We went, Co. A, C, B, Co. F, Co. H, and Co. K. When we got there we found the rebels had left the night before. They left 9 heavy guns and one mortar and 150 Sharps rifles, 150 Carbines. Deserters say there was 1800 men there and 18 field pieces. The bluff was I should think 70 or 80 feet high. They could have sunk any vessel that could have been brought against them. We could not have taken it with infantry. They had only one road to go to it in and they have cannon to sweep that road. It would [have] been almost an impossibility to have taken it at all if they had not been a pack of cowards. This is all the news that I can think of at present. I want to know who is drafted in W. Write if Royal or Albert is either of them drafted. It would kill them I expect to have to go. Tell them if they are drafted to come out to this regiment.... I don't know

*as there is any more signs of its being settled than there was last
spring, it don't seem to me there is.*

November 1862—two short notes

*Dear Mother, I wrote yesterday Uncle Moses was well. He
came in from guard sick I guess. He will get over it. Perhaps we
shall all be at home by spring. If we don't we can't more than die
here. We should have to die if we was to home. It is warm down
here, so warm the boys bathe most every day. It is the first time I
ever bathed in Nov. I must hurry this through as the mail closes
at ten; the steamer goes out today. We expect one in today. I will
take care of myself and try and not get cold. Good by dear Mother
from J K Manchester to L D M*

And on the back side of same paper:

*Nahum and Lidia, I am sick this morning just off from
Guard. Joseph and I, Benjamin all sick in our tent. When we all
come* [home] *Joseph and I shall have some money.*
*Now I send my best respects to you all, to Rebecca
esspeasally. Rebecca, I hope you will answer this to me. Yours in
haste, Moses Austin*

To some it may seem odd that Moses would encourage letter writing between himself and his niece, but perhaps not. Moses was close to
his sister Lydia, who was fourteen years older than he. Her first born,
Eben, was just eight years younger than Moses and very possibly they
were companions. There were logical, familial ties. As the oldest of Lydia's daughters, it seems acceptable that the young adult Rebecca would
correspond with Moses about family news, particularly since he was un-
married and probably would not be receiving mail from too many others. Moreover, his willingness to provide money for a sewing machine
for Rebecca or to assist Nahum and Lydia financially is natural enough
as they were his predominant family connection.

During the June 2012 living history encampment on the Village
Green property of the Windham Historical Society, a member of Civil

War re-enactors of 3rd Maine, Company A explained that garments were not cut to fit; instead three basic sizes were provided, cheaply made, and very often poorly fitting, especially the socks. In this next of Joseph's letters he levels his own complaint regarding U.S. Government issue clothing.

November 16, 1862

Dear Mother, Having a few leisure moments I will spend them writing to you. I am well and rugged as I ever was in my life. The climate agrees with me first rate. It has been very healthy here this summer. There has not been one case of yellow fever here yet. The inhabitants say they never knew the like before. We have lost three men this summer out of our company. Their names were Moses B. Tripp of Buxton, Samuel F. McIntire of Phillips, and Joseph P. Small of Phillips. The rest of the Co are all very well excepting Uncle Benjamin. He can't speak yet. He is pretty smart for him. I think he will be sent home soon. The Col has took it on himself. Uncle Moses has wrote to Rebecca to go to Augusta and get his money. She can get it if she goes there. He says he will pay her expenses if she will go and pay her for her trouble. She need not be one might bashful about going there before strangers. If she don't want to go she can send by anyone that is trusty. Mother you said sometime ago that you would send me some things if I wanted them. I should like to have some things from home. I can get enough here such as they are but they don't suit me at all. The shirts are too large and the socks are good for nothing. One pair of socks such as you knit would wear out three pair of them. If you can send me some shirts and one or two pair of socks I should like it very much. Then I shan't have to draw these government clothes. We have to pay just as much as though they were the best in the world. I want a pair of gloves to handle my gun with. Now it is getting cold weather, send me out a box of things if you can. They will come safe. I should not send for them if I could have got clothes to fit me but I hate to draw clothes that don't fit me nor wear anytime at all. I am going to write Emily on the other side. I will write what little news there is sharing. You can read her letter....

Sister Emily, I will write a few lines to you but you don't deserve to have me write to you at all for you have not wrote to me for a long time. I will write a little of what is going on in this part of the world. The town of St. Mary has been burnt. Two Co,s went over there and the rebels fired on them and wounded one man of Company A. The gunboat Mohawk went up there and shelled the place. The rebels left it after firing a few shots. The gunboat shelled the place untill most night. It was all on fire when she came away. It is in full sight from here. The gunboat was going up there to day if it did not storm to give it to them again. It is no use for them to hang round where we are for we won't allow it. They get drove from every place we go to.

Joseph's story is substantiated by another selection from Chase's history. He had written that "the regiment was on a number of secret raids, one at St. Mary's taking down a mill. A steam-powered sawmill, it was moved to Hilton Head and set up for use there. Later at the same place, as the regiment was withdrawing, the pickets were fired on and one man from Company A was shot. The captain of the gunboat that was protecting the troops gave notice to the mayor of the place to remove the women and children from it as he was going to open fire on the place, which he did."[6] Chase also acknowledged that "the regiment was engaged in digging up cannon on the mainland at the south of Amelia Island."[7]

Joseph continues:

The other day the Darlington, a steamer we took here, went over where the rebel salt works is and broke up all of their kettles and brought away about 15 bushels of salt and set fire to the buildings and burnt them all down. That Schooner that our Company was watching has been captured by the gunboat Hale. There was two of them in there. They burned one and brought the other away with them....

Tell father I want him to write an order for me to draw my pay here. That is all the way the captain says we can get it. Write it and send it in the next letter. I have got one of them roses I spoke about. I am going to send it to you. The name of it is the

pride of Florida. I can't think of anything more at present so good
by from your brother J. K. Manchester to E. J.

Joseph's regiment was not without its pranksters…

> *November 28ᵗʰ 1862*
> *Dear Sister,… I should have wrote before but it has been all*
> *hurry and preparation for Thanksgiving which was yesterday. We*
> *had a fine dinner, I tell you, for soldiers are not supposed to have*
> *such days to themselves. You wrote news that I did not expect to*
> *hear; now you must not blame me if I do laugh a little, just one*
> *ha ha?… Uncle Moses says he never asked you to marry him in*
> *any of his letters. He says nothing was farther from his thoughts*
> *than that. He says if anyone wrote such a letter as you wrote me*
> *he did, it must be some one got hold of his writing and copied it.*
> *I know some one wrote a letter to a girl in Denmark and signed*
> *my name to it and I got an answer back. What do [you] think of*
> *that? I did not know any such a person in the world; perhaps the*
> *same one that wrote the letter for me wrote to you. I say it may*
> *be so but perhaps it aint so. He says all he ever wrote that you*
> *could infer that from was in the beginning of his letters, and that*
> *was Dear friend Rebecca. He feels very bad about it; he wants*
> *you to let me know if you have received the watch he sent you.*
> *He says he shall never write again while he is in the service until*
> *he finds out who wrote the letter. Enough of this. Rebecca, I want*
> *you to send me some postage stamps [even] if you have to go to*
> *Portland to get them. I forgot to tell you I got the papers this time.*
> *Tell mother I shant be able to answer her letter today but I will*
> *answer her questions. George Nason got here in the last boat; we*
> *got 5 recruits with him. George is well⁸ and rugged and also the*
> *rest of the Windham boys.*

…or its rumormongers:

> *Dec 25, 1862*
> *Dear Father and Mother, I take my pen in hand to inform*
> *you that my health is good at present. I received a letter from*

home today bearing date Dec 5th and another dated Nov 29th I was glad to hear from home. I am always glad to know you all are well. Little Seward wrote about my sheep and lambs. Libby boys had a letter from home stating that I wrote home that the Regt was destitute of clothing. I did not write so, and I must correct it. I want you to tell the Libbys that it is not so, that I did not write so. We have clothes enough such as they are but they don't fit; I want some smaller that is all. If I get some that fit me from home that will save me from drawing them. I don't want to take clothes that don't fit and that is why that I wrote for them. Elbridge has started it. Nice story but I want it stopt.

To his father specifically:

Mother says you are jealous. She says you think I think more of her than I do of you. I think as much of one as I do of the other but mother writes more to me than you do. That is why I write to her so much more than I do the rest. That is all foolishness to take notice of that. About the order—that is right enough but you did not state when my pay was to commence here. I shall have to do that to suit myself. I am very glad you have got my sheep. Keep them as you and I talked of before I came away. Tell Emily I can't answer her letter tonight as it is most dark. Tell her it was very gladly received and read with interest. Tell her I will send her some more flowers as I can find some she has not seen. Uncle Ben is coming home in the first boat that leaves here. He will bring some things that I am going to send.

Centered at the very end of the letter he writes in beautiful script and large letters:

Christmas Eve

Chapter 8

HILTON HEAD

In January 1863, the 9th Maine returned to Hilton Head, 10th Corp., Department of the South.[1] The next series of posts come from there. On February 3 Joseph mentions his present good health, thanks his father for the stamps, and indicates how pleased he is with the box of clothing that had arrived.

> *My clothes that I had in the box are just what I want. I couldn't have made a better selection if I had picked them out myself. I shant need more right away; when I want more I will write for them.*

Also, he is irritated with Elbridge for having started the rumor about the regiment's lack of clothing. Stephen is Elbridge's younger brother, about Joseph's age.

> *E. Libby don't have much to say now to me. I don't want anything to do with him. He ain't one of my kind. Stephen is good enough. He uses me first rate....*
>
> *We are having a rain storm now. I was detailed for guard this morning but it rained so I haven't been on guard yet. We expect to be paid of soon. The paymaster is here with the money. I shall send you some as soon as I get it. It has been six months since we was paid of. If I can get my money by this order I shall send it to you by express. It will be the safest way. I must write to mother.*

Joseph is greatly appreciative of the clothes and says so to each of his parents; moreover, he tells his mother of his attempt at free enterprise.

> *Dear Mother,... I was very glad of the clothes, they are very good ones, just what I want. I shant need any more for a good while to come. You spoke of Uncle Moses writing. He is lame in the hospital with the rheumatism. Uncle Benjamin has gone home. He has got home by this time. When you see him he will tell what kind of a boy I am. I can't think of much more to write but I will tell you how the prices are out here. Butter is 40 cts, Cheese is 20 cts, flour is 25 cts per pound, Raisons 40cts, and so other things to match. Apples is 4 dollars a barrel. I bought a barrel and sold out by the dollar's worth. I made about 4 dollars on them. I shall get another barrel tomorrow. If I had enough out here to trade on I could make more than I get from government. I should have made more on them but half of them was rotten.*

Joseph begins this next letter using the charming, stylistic convention of the period. The pleasant weather of Fernandina has given way to raw cold in South Carolina.

> *Feb 6, 1863*
>
> *Dear Sister Rebecca, I improve the time set before me now by writing to you to inform you of my health which is good at present. I wrote to Father and Mother but the mail did not go so I thought I would write or rather scribble a few lines to you and Emily. It has rained incessantly for some days past, making it very uncomfortable for us soldiers in the small tents, scarce room enough to turn round in without hitting the side of the tent and getting wet through. This is a southern winter, part of the time cold enough to freeze you and then again the wind blowing the sand so you are in danger of losing both eyes if you venture out doors. Pleasant country to live in. Delightfull Climate don't you think so? Charming weather, I think, but never mind; all things have an end (my bible says). There will be an end to this sometime or other, sooner or later. I will wait patiently for it. It is all we can do is to wait. We are laying here doing nothing as usual. There is an expedition fitting out here to attack Charleston or Savannah,*

it is hard to tell which. It is all secret. We are so nigh them there might be afries right among us so there is nothing said about it that anyone can get hold of.... Joe K M [This is the only letter where Joseph signs his name as "Joe."]

The word *afries* as Joseph used it refers to slaves, or Africans, and his thinking is that nearby slaves who were loyal to their owners might tip them off about the planned port city attacks; hence, the secrecy.

Perhaps it is useful to explain here that during January 20–23 a strong rain event stalled Union forces under the command of General Ambrose Burnside. Cold, followed by the unexpected spell of rain, had turned the frozen roads to mud. Apparently Joseph and his buddies are encountering similarly miserable weather in early February, though Joseph is resolved to maintain his upbeat perspective about it.

To Emily, even though he has almost nothing to say, he jots a few lines. Ironically, the last sentence is historically interesting.

I think I will write to you now as I have time and opportunity. I did not know but what you would be jealous if I wrote to the rest and did not write to you. I have wrote the news in Res' letter, read that. So I must think of something else to write you. You must excuse me if I don't write much for I am at a loss what to write. There is nothing doing to make a subject to write on, so you see what a condition I am in. All there is now for us to do is to play ball, a good occupation for soldiers.

More than likely Joseph is referring to the game of baseball. It originated in games from England called "cricket" or "rounders," among others, and came to America with the first colonists, where over time many variations and many new names emerged. In New England it became known as "townball" or "baseball" and sometimes "round ball," from running around the bases.

Rules of 1861 were significantly different from those of today. For examples: 1) home plate was round, like a plate; 2) baseball gloves were not used; 3) the umpire did not call balls or strikes; 4) a batter was out if the fielder caught the ball on the first bounce, but runners still could advance. At the beginning of the Civil War, the game was mainly a Northerner's activity, but with the spread of Northern troops into the South, so spread the game of baseball. As Joseph's letters attest, when not on duty or in combat, there was much boredom and down time; thus, to fill in those intervals, soldiers played ball. Because the game needed only some sort of bat, makeshift items to use for bases, and a ball, the game traveled readily and could be played almost anywhere. It was played on parade grounds inside forts, on large spaces near encampments close to battle-fields where Southern pickets could observe, and by Northern soldiers in Southern prison camps. In such a manner, the game of baseball eventu-ally became the national pastime.

On February 14, 1863, Joseph makes a point of sending his mother $10.00 *ten dollars for your own use and no one else, for I think you must want some but you wouldn't tell me perhaps. I don't want you to keep any of it for me if you want it yourself. I am young and can do without the money better then you can. I put 15 in father's letter. If it gets to him safe I shall send more to him.*

Elsewhere in his short note, he asks *to know just how things stand at home, don't keep back a thing from me....* [As usual, he is curious about the ventures and labors at the farm.] *Seward said father had bought my sheep. Tell me if they have got any lambs and how many.*

This next inclusion is from Moses Austin to Lydia. While his words and spelling are simple, they reflect his overall good-hearted intentions as well as the disdain he has for his brother Benjamin and the physical pain his forty-two-year-old body is experiencing. The offense he writes of perhaps relates to the reference in Joseph's earlier letter about Mo-ses having no marriage intentions regarding Rebecca or of his writing her ever again. Moses also provides one of the few third-person insights about Joseph and the very fine young man he is.

Hilton Head SC Feb 26, 1863
Dear Sister Lydia, I thought I would rite a line to you. I hope I shal not offend you as I did Rebecca. Tel Rebecca I am sorry that I offended her and should bee glad to hear from her. I am sick in the Hosbittle and I do not know how it will turn with me. I understand that Rebecca has not received that watch I sent to her by William Mitchel but I shall see that she has it. Tel Mary that I shal make her a presant when I return. I have ben in the

hosbittle 2 months sick. My hand trembles so you must excuse this riting.

Give my best wishes to all of your friends. Has Benjamin paid you what he owed Joseph? If he has not he has not treated Joseph wright but it is as well as he ever treats anyone. He owes me money that I lent him but Joseph is a good boy and it is not wright for him to be used in such a manner. Lydia I feel so unwell that I must close for this time. I want all of you to rite as often as you can.

From Moses Austin Give this 10 cent bill to Alice as a presant from me.

Moses's gift calls for a side note. As the war continued, hoarding of small coins developed, and by 1862 the government countered with ten-cent and twenty-five-cent paper currencies. Similar in look to today's one dollar bill, the ten-cent bill featured green printing and bore the likeness of George Washington.

In his very clear, lovely, and easy-to-read handwriting, Moses pens a letter to Rebecca after all, and to some extent an unflattering picture of Rebecca emerges from between the lines. After the marriage embarrassment mentioned in Joseph's earlier letters, he now addresses her as "Respected Niece Rebecca." With no great need to spend his pay on himself or to send it home to a wife and family, Moses is accumulating money and is generous in sharing it with his sister and her family.

Hilton Head Port Royal March 11, 1863

Respected Niece Rebecca, After reading a part of Joseph's letter I seat myself to rite a line to you. Rebecca you left off riting to me so suddin that I made up my mind that you was frunted with me and I thought best for me not to rite any more. But I am very sorry that I roat any thing to put you out with me for I did not intend to do so. You told Joseph to tel me to send you money to buy a sewing machine if I had a mind to. You might roate to me yourself for the money. I can let you have 60 Dollars if it will help you any. I am just as willing to accomidate you now as I was before you got frunted with me. But I will not say any more about that ~~ But you can have what money you want to buy that Machiene with. You say 60 Dollars will Buy it. Rebecca, after you answer this letter I will cend it to you. My Money is all in 10 Dollar Bills and when I send it to you I shal put 3 10 Dollar Bills in Each letter. I shal rite 2 letters to you and each letter will contain 30 Dollars so you will know how to look for it. I have a Hundred Dollars that I carry in my Pockett evry Day for I have no other place to put it ~~ I have ben sick in the hosbittle most 3 months but I am little better to night.

Rebecca, Give my love to All of your folks. Moses Austin to Rebecca E Manchester

About three weeks later Rebecca receives another letter from Hilton Head, this time from her brother. Joseph's writings detail circumstances and events that resonate with New England expression. His news-filled letter is written April 3, 1863. Just as Fernandina, Florida, was an easy ten months or so without much rebel activity, the reverse is true in the Hilton Head, South Carolina, area.

We are encamped in the woods about 6 miles from head quarters doing outpost duty. We have been out here about two months. We have lost 4 men since we have been here. The rebels came over one foggy night and took them prisoners, but they haven't got me yet nor I don't mean they shall right away. I don't know but what they will get the whole of our Regiment by piecemeal if they keep on in this way. They have got 25 or so of them already and they haven't got more than 4 or 5 at a time yet. The expedition against Charleston has gone. They will attack them as soon as the wind is favorable. The wind blows hard every day. They cannot fight to advantage when the wind blows. There is no other news at present. The boys are all well and rugged. What does Uncle Moses say about letting you have the money to buy a sewing machine with? He told me he could let you have the whole amount and I think he will if you keep the right side of him. Have you heard from Uncle Ben lately? Let me know how he is getting along. Find out if he can talk yet. He couldn't speak a loud word when he went away from here then.

4th ... the expedition against Charleston have taken James

Island. That is one great step toward taking Charleston for Jas Island was covered with cannon. I commenced writing this letter last night but had to go on guard so I could not finish it until tonight.... I have been asleep most all day and I don't feel much like writing so you must excuse this scribbling.

Ever since the initial stages of the Civil War, an ongoing Northern strategy had been to close Southern ports, thereby providing economic strangulation and preventing wartime commerce in the form of artillery, munitions, supplies, and necessities. The plan met with successes in 1861, for Union forces were able to capture coastal forts and sea islands and establish supply centers and coastline control; but by spring of 1863, the Union Navy still could not wrap its arms around the big prize, the seizing of Confederate-held Fort Sumter and the subsequent sealing off of Charleston Harbor. An attempt had been made on April 7, but it failed dismally as harbor "torpedoes" (mines anchored under water), rope netting, logs, and other obstructions were difficult to clear in order that Union ironclads—challenging to maneuver—could penetrate the harbor. Casualty of that harbor conflict was the *USS Keokuk*, an ironclad steamer commissioned just a month earlier in March 1863. Her design, both experimental and odd, was no match for the nearly one hundred Confederate projectiles that struck her, and she was forced to withdraw. The next morning the *Keokuk* sank off Morris Island. The *Keokuk* story does not end there, however. Because the *Keokuk* had sunk in shallow water, her smokestack was visible, and in the dark and stealth of night, in a remarkable engineering feat, Confederates salvaged the two eleven-inch guns from the wreck. Unfortunately for the later Battery Wagner assault, Confederates also had retrieved a signal book, and with it the key to breaking the Federal code.[2] The Union game plan soon would be in Confederate hands and to Union disadvantage.[3]

Chapter 9

ST. HELENA

Early in June 1863, the 9th Maine was moved from Hilton Head to St. Helena Island, a few miles north of Hilton Head and closer to Morris Island and Charleston Harbor. Over the previous two months the planning and determination to take Charleston had intensified, as indicated in Joseph's letter. Evident also is his continued resolve to see the war through. Still, since that September day in 1861 when he first left for Augusta, he has not seen his family and a whisper of longing infuses his words. From St. Helena he writes to Emily on June 10, but first he has to chide her.

> It has been some time since I rec'd a letter from you and I had begun to think you had forgot your Soldier Brother but I think you haven't quite yet. At least I hope you haven't. I have just got off guard and my nerves are not very still as you can see by my writing. I got a letter from you and mother last night and I was very glad to hear father was getting along so well with his spring's work. I should like to be at home to help him. I expect he wishes so too but I can't get there so I must wait another year. Then I can be there but I shall see this war done away with before I come. You may be assured of that. I enlisted to put down or at least to do what I could toward it and I am bound to see it through before I come home. I don't know how that may suit you at home but that is my determination. If nothing happens to me I shall get a furlough if I can. I think I can get one in Aug or Sept but I can't get one before that. I don't think the furloughs are stopt for a short time in this depart[mt] There is going to be a change of troops in this depart[mt] soon we have every reason to believe. We have been

here about 18 months and they don't think it best for us to stay through the warm weather here.

Stephen Wise confirms in his book, *Gate of Hell, Campaign for Charleston Harbor, 1863,* what Joseph next avers about the hottest and most sickly months of the year in South Carolina. He cites James Seddon, secretary of war for the Confederacy, who had ordered his General (Pierre Toutant Gustave) Beauregard to send units away from Charleston and Savannah to aid elsewhere. Beauregard protested but Seddon persisted, maintaining that the "near approach of your sickly season and the present sultry weather" would deter any serious threats to Charleston.[1]

It is as warm here now as it is in Maine in July. Next month and August will be the two hottest months and the most sickly ones but if we use proper precautions there is no more to be feared than there is at home. A man must not eat any salt pork nor any fried beef, but he must eat all the sweet potatoes, watermelons, and such green stuff as that will prevent the scurvy. We have got to shade our tents with palmetto or vines. That will make them very cool and nice and we are ordered to fish in the morning and eve and to bathe twice a week in the salt water. That will do a great deal towards the men's health. The men are as willing to bathe as the Generals are to have us so if that will promote the men's health, is no danger but what we shall be healthy. The Libbys are well as usual. George is well. He is hostler now. He is in the best chance that there is in this Reg't and I am glad for him.

He next tells of Uncle Moses, who is working on machinery designed to better remove harbor hazards.

Uncle Moses is well. He is over here to work on a machine to get it ready for action. It is designed to draw out the spiles and torpedoes and other obstructions in Charles harbor and other places. It is a large square bowed steamer with lifting power riged on the bows to catch the rebel machines in the water. When it is ready to work I have no doubt but what it will take every thing out of the channel so our monitors can go there without getting blowed out of the water. There is a network of cable across the harbor. If that is cut, the monitors can go right up to Fort Sumter so snug that they [Fort Sumter Confederates] *can't bring a gun to bear on them* [Union monitors]. *They* [Confederate guns] *are so low then the monitors can batter the fort down at there pleasure. The monitors don't have much to fear from torpedoes for they are generaly sunk from 8 to ten feet below the surface and the ironclads draw from 5 to seven and 8 feet. Most of them* [Union ships] *will run over them* [torpedoes] *without touching them. The rebels made great calculations thinking that the torpedoes would sink every ironclad that we had, but they will find out that yankee ingenuity can invent a machine that will remove there southern bulldogs as they term they* [their] *harbor defenses. There is one of them lies at anchor off here. It is the Weehawken, the one that led the fight before the Keokuk run by her. The marks of the fight show pretty plainly on her deck and turret.*

The *Weehawken* led the Union fleet in its April 7 assault with a device fitted to her bow to clear the obstructed harbor.[2] She was hit more than fifty times and a naval mine exploded beneath her, though it did not inflict serious damage. Unable to navigate the harbor and under Confederate guns, the fleet withdrew within an hour. The *Weehawken* was readily repaired and placed back in service as Joseph indicates next.

She is going out soon. [The Weehawken left that day for an expected engagement in Georgia.] *There is a Brig along side of her loaded with ammunition, dealing out powder and PILLS for the southern confed—dose one PILL to 10 REBELS taken at intervals of about 3 to a minute. I think that is about right for their case. Some of them need medical attendance very much. Such ones as Myers, J Davis, Beauregard, Floyd[3] and a host of others too numerous to mention.*

As Joseph wraps up this letter, he makes a point of mentioning those at home, especially the younger ones. Joseph's many letters indicate his own propensity for reading, learning, self-improvement, and good behavior. Where they refer to Seward especially, Joseph almost always reminds him to be a good and helpful boy and to pursue learning. Joseph himself is cleverly humorous and disarming.

> *I guess you will think I am in a hurry by the way this letter is wrote but I haven't taken any pains with this and if you can read it you can do better than I can for I don't believe I could read it over myself if I should try. You must excuse this short letter and poor writing. Give my love to all who enquire after me and accept the same yourself. You have my miniature so you can tell how I look (the same homly Joe that I was at home). Tell father to do the best he can. Tell mother she is not forgotten either. Tell Seward he must be a good boy and go to school all he can. You can let him read this if he can. Tell Alice she must not think hard of me because I don't write to her oftener. I can [not] think of any more noncense to write so I must close. Good by from your brother Joseph to Emily. Direct as before.*

> *St. Helena   June 14ʰ 63*
> *We have just got off inspection & my hand is unsteady. It is very warm here. It makes me sweat like a Beaver as the saying is. This morning when I went to pack my knapsack for inspection I found some light fingered rogue had relieved me of 3 pair of socks, among them one pair that come from home that I wouldn't taken no money for. They took all but the pair I had on. Isn't that a shame? I am sorry that there is such men in the Regt but there is too many of them. I would like to have you send me one or two (Prs) by mail if you can. The government socks are very poor. If you can send me some I want you to knit the initials of my name in them. Then they won't dare to steal them; if they do they will be found out. I sent a paper to Seward yesterday. Let me know if he received it; it is directed to him. I am coming on furlough if possible. The furloughs are suspended for a time. I don't know how long, probably they will commence again soon. Now we have got another Gen in this department; Gen Gilmore commands this department. I think he will do something. He is more go ahead than Hunter. I want to get home this summer if possible. I am*

tired of staying in one place all the time. It is tiresome to us, but if we are doing any good staying on these Islands I am contented to stay our term of service out here. But I can't see as we are doing any good at all. There is no news at all, only a negro company had a riot day before yesterday and they brought them all in irons to the head. They looked meaken, I tell you. They won't do much in this part of the country. They are too lazy. They don't want to do anything at all. They will lay down & go to sleep right in the blazing sun. It would scorch us to death in five minutes. But enough of this. Ask Rebecca if she ever means to write to me again. When did you hear from Eben? I haven't heard from him for a long time. Must close by bidding you good by from your Son Joseph K. Manchester to Mrs. L. D. Manchester

Actually, there was news. Stephen Wise explains that under command of James Montgomery, troops entered the town of Darien, Georgia, on the June 10 mission, and detachments from each regiment, both the white and now the newly established African-American troops, were ordered to break into houses to collect food and other useful items as well as to plunder thoroughly.[4] Colonel Robert Shaw, who had trained the 54th Massachusetts regiment, "was outraged" that his U.S. Colored Troops would have "to participate in such activities and immediately began writing letters to Massachusetts Governor Andrew and others to help him free the 54th from such duty."[5] For Governor John A. Andrew, Windham, Maine, native, "creation of the black regiment had been his dream"[6] and the 54th Massachusetts was his "pet regiment."[7] Gov. Andrew wrote to Brig. General David Hunter, who "considered the raids honorable work and did not take the 54th away from Montgomery, but Shaw's men were never again used in such a manner."[8] Five weeks later Colonel Shaw and the 54th valiantly would lead the charge on Battery Wagner.

While there are no letters to support this supposition, it may be that the Negro riots two days earlier of which Joseph had written were related to the expedition in Georgia; also, as Joseph had indicated, General Hunter was replaced by General Quincy Gillmore to command the Department of the South. The exchange of generals occurred on June 12.

St Helena So C   June 26, 1863

Dear father, I now take my pen in hand to inform you of my health which is good at present and I hope these few lines will find you enjoying the same blessing. There is no news of importance here at present but what you have heard probably. Most every thing of interest is the Rebel man captured in Warsaw Sound where you remember our Brigade was encamped just before we took Fernandina Florida. The particulars will probably be in the papers so it is no use for me to write them.

We are having a fine time here. The weather is pretty warm but we are used to it now and it doesn't effect us much. Now we have about three hours a day drill; the rest of the time we do as we please in our quarters. The Regt is out drilling now but I got excused today. The boys are well and in fine spirits now. We shall have a Gen inspection and services tomorrow by Brig Gen Gilmore, commanding the Department of the South. We some expect to move to Folly Island nearer Charleston. We shall probably see some fighting soon if we don't participate in it, but we are in good condition for a fight as we ever was; there is over 900 men in the Regt now. There is no sick ones, hardly every one in the hospital is well enough to eat at the mess table. There isn't many regts that can say that.

Joseph's reason for confidence is sustained again by Stephen Wise. Brigadier General George C. Strong, arriving on June 17, was chosen to lead the assault. Strong "worked [the troops] constantly, both under the hot sun and in rainstorms, marching on the loose island sand. Strong was determined his brigade be prepared."[9]

I want you to write oftener to me. I don't get a letter from you once in a dog's age.

He also hopes for mail from his Aunt Ruth, whom he wrote a long time ago; Mrs. Ester Prince, who promised to write; and his cousins, Nahum and William. None of them have written back.

He asks about his cousins, Nahum and William. *Has either of [them] enlisted? ... I shall send you the account of the capture of the rebel ram which may interest you some.*

Poignantly, he says to his father, *try for the best until I get at home; then I guess we can carry things along to advantage. Do not let mother expose herself any if possible.* [His concern for their well-being and financial condition is all but palpable and he is determined to require as little money as possible for himself so that he can better support their needs.] *I shall do as well as I can with my money until I have sent home all I could out of my thirteen dollars per month. I have been as saving as possible with my money. There isn't many privates that has saved more money than I have, but enough of this talk.*

I can't write much more this time. Please write as soon as you can get this and write all the news. I received some papers this mail. They was very interesting. Send them to me as fast as you can; after I read them the boys all want to borrow them. Papers are in good demand. Uncle Moses is well; he is at work at the Head; he has 40 cts a day extra. He is coming on furlough if he can get one.

He continues his mantra about education and counsels Nahum to *tell Seward to be a good boy until I get home. Let him go to school all you can spare him; you never will be sorry for it. Good bye from your son Joseph K Manchester to N Manchester*

While Joseph was recalling his company's health, the regiment's size, light fingers, possible furloughs, rebels, newspapers, and Uncle Moses, General Quincy Gillmore and Rear Admiral John Dahlgren were devising strategy for the combined land and sea assault on Morris Island, seen as the gateway to overcoming Fort Sumter and establishing a blockade of Charleston. The plan of operations was to take the south end of Morris Island first, with troop movement northward to lay siege to and overcome Battery Wagner, which was about a mile and a half from Fort Sumter. Battery Gregg at Cummings Point also was a target, and with both of these Confederate-held properties under Union control, the combined land and sea forces could incapacitate Fort Sumter. With Fort Sumter unable to fire on Union ships, the ironclads could enter the channel, remove the harbor obstructions, and cut off Charleston. That was the plan.

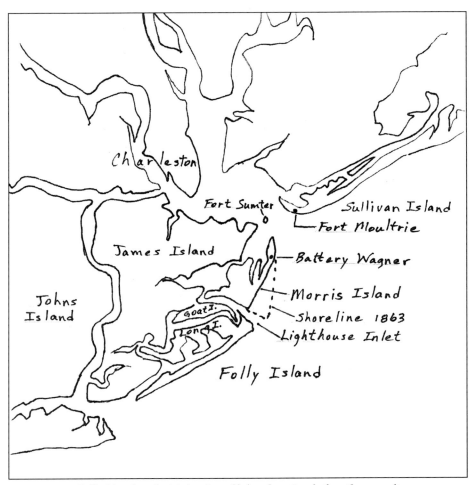

*Folly Island and vicinity, Joseph's last location before the assault
of Battery Wagner on Morris Island*

Chapter 10

FOLLY ISLAND

J oseph would write next from Folly Island on Tuesday, July 7, 1863. It would be his last letter.

Dear Parents, I will now improve this opportunity by writing you a few lines to inform you of my whereabouts which is you see at Folly Island. I don't know how far it is to Charleston from here but we are near enough to hear their drums beat. We are concealed in the woods about 400 yds from Morris Island. We expect to attack them. Every day our troops are waiting for orders to march. At present we have got batteries built within 400 yds of the Rebels' lines that they don't know anything about. All that remains now is to cut the bushes down in front and open on them. Then is fun ahead and work too. We are ready for them. I expect we have got to storm the batteries and take them at the point of the bayonet. The rebels have got to pick up or else we have. We are all well as usual. Elbridge is writing to his folks. The men are in fine spirits. We shall get new rifles this week, the Col says. I hope we shall for these we have got is no better than they should be for such a case as this. I suppose before you get this letter we shall either have Morris I or we shall get repulsed there. At any rate we are going to try it. I may be shot in battle but you may be ashured I shall do my duty as far forward as I can. There is no news at present to write about, therefore it is hard to make up a letter. We are having a good time now laying in the shade of these trees. No one would ever know there was 15,000 [actually 5340][1] *men laying behind these banks. The rebels don't know that we are here, for their sentries walk on their batteries within easy rifle shot of us. If they knew that we was here they wouldn't show themselves you may depend. I don't want you to borrow any trouble about me. Do the best you can without me until I get home; I make calculation about getting home again. I don't worry in the least about my welfare. Can't think of any more this time. I hope the next time we have a chance to write it will be in the City of C, or the batteries on Morris Island. Excuse this poor writing for I am in a hurry to pitch my tent. Give my love to all who enquire after me. Accept the best respects of your son.* [In a large, curlicue box,] *Tell Seward to be a good boy as he can.*

Joseph K Manchester [in signature] *to Nahum Manchester, L D Manchester*

Although Joseph believed "the rebels don't know we are here," Stephen Wise writes that Confederates suspected an imminent attack: an observation balloon reported transports in the roads at Port Royal, a July 8 scouting party up Folly Creek spotted small boats and construction, and intercepted messages indicated preparation of barges and cutters off Folly Island.[2] Since Joseph's 9th Maine was among the regiments of Strong's brigade, several excerpts from Wise's text provide probable accounts of Joseph's activity following his July 7 letter home. The passages were selected only as they may relate to Joseph; for a detailed and compelling study of the battles and their background, the reader is encouraged to read Stephen R. Wise's book, *Gate of Hell, Campaign for Charleston Harbor, 1863.*

> While waiting for the navy, the army's contingent was organized for action. Commanders ordered regimental cooks to prepare three days' rations for the men. On July 8, the soldiers of Strong's brigade were put through rigorous final inspections. At the same time, a white flannel strip was sewn on the left sleeve of every soldier so that friend might be distinguished from foe in the night attack.[3]
>
> At nightfall of July 8 … the men on Folly Island marched to barges waiting in the Folly River. The loading was long and tiresome. For almost the entire night Strong's men waited in silence, some in boats, some on shore.… Finally, toward dawn,

word was passed that the attack had been called off. Disgusted, the tired soldiers returned to their camps.

Gillmore had canceled the assault because the naval launches, delayed by a heavy squall, had not reached the rendezvous point on time, and his engineers had failed to cut sufficient passageways through the Confederate obstructions in the Folly River.... Gillmore made plans to proceed with the attack the following morning.[4]

General Strong's brigade, again sitting in launches on that hot July 10 morning, could hear (and feel) the crossfire of the monitors' guns and Confederate cannons. "The noise of the bombardment was so great that it was heard at the Union base in Port Royal, more than fifty miles away."[5]

Slowly, the Union soldiers through bursting shells, worked their boats nearer and nearer. Leading the way was the 7th Connecticut, followed by the 6th Connecticut, 3rd New Hampshire, 76th Pennsylvania, 9th Maine, and four companies of the 48th New York. As the distance to Morris Island shortened, the Federals found that the Southerners could not depress their guns enough and their shells were whistling harmlessly overhead, but just as they escaped the cannon fire, the Confederate soldiers in the rifle pits began a rapid fusillade.

Still, Strong ordered his men ashore ... and all the regiments, except Colonel Chatfield's 6th Connecticut, obeyed...[6]

Strong directed the rest of his units against the rifle pits. First ashore were skirmishers armed with seven-shot Spencer rifles. Then, regiment after regiment, with bayonets fixed, clamored out of their boats, formed in knee-deep mud and began wading inland. Strong, anxious to join the fray, leaped from his boat before it landed and disappeared under the water, only his hat floating on the waves, but he soon surfaced, reached shore, stripped off his waterlogged boots and began directing the attack. Pausing to fire volleys, the Northerners continued to press on, and soon the lead regiment, the 7th Connecticut, reached the rifle pits where they engaged in heavy hand-to-hand fighting.[7]

Confederate rifle pits at Light House Inlet—the southern end of Morris Island and opposite end of Battery Wagner—having been surrounded, Southern units retreated to Battery Wagner, relinquishing the pits. Monitors continued to bombard the island and at the end of the day, the Union would count the conflict as a victory for its side. While troops had captured three-fourths of the island, the day's work and the unbearable heat had exhausted the landing troops, however, and the day-long naval engagement had left the sailors on the monitors likewise exhausted from their continuous ordeal, both above and below decks.

Strong's rigorous inspections attest to Joseph's belief that his company was ready and in fine spirits; the regiments likely had been instructed about and prepared to use their bayonets as Joseph also had mentioned. Standard issue during the Civil War were muzzle-loading rifled muskets with bayonets, which still were critical to hand-to-hand conflict.

In the foggy, pre-dawn hours of July 11, an attack was launched on Battery Wagner itself. Emboldened by the success of the previous day, only three regiments were engaged: the 7th Connecticut, the 76th Pennsylvania, and the 9th Maine. In summary, the 7th Connecticut was trapped on the slopes of Wagner and Confederate fire assailed the Pennsylvania and Maine units that followed, ultimately preventing them from coming to the aid and rescue of their Connecticut brethren.

For the 7th Connecticut, 13 were killed, 29 wounded, 61 missing. For the 76th Pennsylvania, 35 killed, 123 wounded, 83 missing. For the 9th Maine, 1 killed, 32 wounded, 23 missing.[8] The one soldier killed from the 9th Maine was Stephen Libby,[9] Joseph's friend and Elbridge's brother.

Realizing that an assault on Battery Wagner needed more than manpower behind it, General Gillmore had breaching batteries constructed over the course of the next week, a week of heat, rain, and mosquitoes.[10] The batteries would be armed with siege guns and mortars. Confederate General P. T. G. Beauregard also was gearing up.

During the dark night hours of the 16th, drenching storms thundered and lit up the skies, and rain on the 17th forced postponement of the dual-pronged naval and land strike planned for that day. Heavy rains persisted through the early morning of Saturday the 18th as well, but Gillmore and Dahlgren went ahead with the planned attack, beginning with constant firing of missiles from the monitors. "While the Northern gunners believed their shells were ripping Battery Wagner apart, in actuality little damage was done to the battery or its garrison. The sand fort was able to absorb the punishment and protect its garrison."[11] This is not to say that the guns had little effect, however, for masses of sand and shells filling in the battery and blocking passageways hindered and exhausted the Confederates as they tried to keep the battery functioning.

In the dusk of evening, the bombardment stilled as the infantry under Gillmore's authorization readied to charge the outer walls of Battery Wagner. Maps depicting Morris Island in 1865 indicate a narrow strip of land and marshways that channeled the regiments onto an even narrower strip of sand a few hundred feet wide as they approached Battery Wagner. Because Gillmore, overconfident and terribly misguided, believed the day's shelling had successfully damaged Wagner; because the Confederates, having previously retrieved the code book from the *Keokuk*, could break the code and determine the strategy; and because the Southerners had surreptitiously reinforced the battery with both men and heavy munitions, the fighting was fierce and decimating.

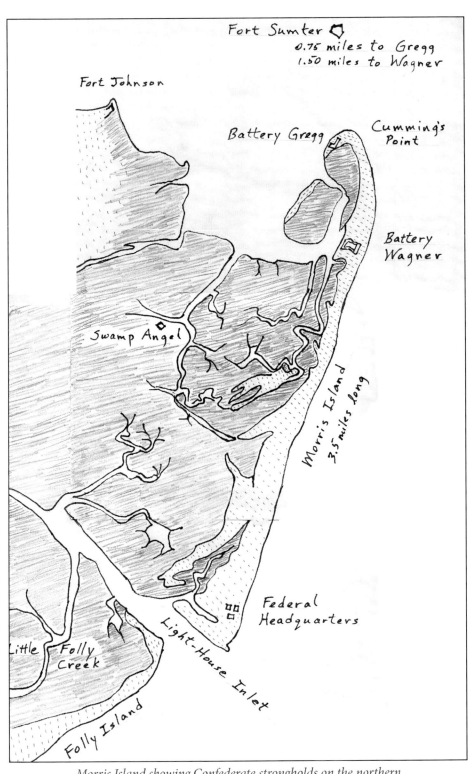

Fort Sumter
0.75 miles to Gregg
1.50 miles to Wagner

Fort Johnson

Battery Gregg

Cumming's Point

Battery Wagner

Swamp Angel

Morris Island 3.5 miles long

Federal Headquarters

Little Folly Creek

Light-House Inlet

Folly Island

Morris Island showing Confederate strongholds on the northern end of the island and Union-held sectors to the south

Chapter 11

BATTERY WAGNER, MORRIS ISLAND

At 7:45 p.m., Colonel Robert Gould Shaw led his Massachusetts 54th regiment of free African-American soldiers—made famous in the award-winning motion picture *Glory*—on foot; they were armed only with fixed bayonets while volleys from within Wagner and cannon from without "cut huge gaps in the attacking formation."[1] Still, under the leadership of Colonel Shaw, the remaining 54th reached and scaled the sand-and-log embankment. Strong's brigade, comprised of the 76th Pennsylvania, the 9th Maine, and the 3rd New Hampshire, advanced at 8:45 p.m. to support Shaw's 54th troops. Following the command of Colonel John H. Jackson, the 3rd New Hampshire led the regiments of Strong's brigade toward Wagner,[2] coming "under a rain of shot, canister, grape, and shell,"[3] tearing "severe gaps into the ranks of the 3rd New Hampshire and the following 9th Maine and the 76th Pennsylvania."[4] General Strong would lead the survivors on to Wagner, but recognizing the hopelessness of the situation soon thereafter, he stood on an embankment to issue the order to retreat. In so doing, he was mortally wounded in the thigh and died twelve days later. In horrific, bloody, hand-to-hand struggle with Wagner's defenders in the meantime, the 54th would occupy a section of the fort briefly, but would be forced to withdraw. The casualty list of the 54th alone would record 34 killed, 146 wounded, and 92 missing.[5] Their greatly respected leader Colonel Shaw would be among the several officers who fell among his men. Of the 500[6] men from the 9th Maine, the casualty list recorded 4 killed, 94 wounded, and 19 missing.[7] Joseph K. Manchester, with a bullet in his right shoulder, was among the injured.

While it is widely known that Clara Barton founded the American Red Cross and that she arranged for supplies and provided nursing care to soldiers in the field during the Civil War, it is lesser known, perhaps, that she was on Morris Island during the Union assault of Battery Wagner. Having arrived on July 14, she established a camp on the southern end of the island.[8] "With the doctors, Clara Barton forwarded the wounded to a field hospital near Light-House Inlet where, because the Federals feared an enemy counterattack, they were immediately placed on small steamers and sent to Stono Inlet. There they were transferred to the hospital ship *Cosmopolitan* and taken to hospitals at Hilton Head and Beaufort."[9] Joseph was taken to General Hospital No. 2 in Beaufort, about seventy miles away.

PHOTOGRAPHS

Nahum Manchester

Seward Manchester,
Joseph's youngest brother,
around age 45

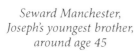

The farmhouse in 1888, very much as Joseph would have known it. In the photo are Nahum and Lydia, Seward and Ida, and their children.

The farmhouse roughly 100 years later.
Courtesy David Manchester

Boody's Store and Post Office
Courtesy of Windham Historical Society

Main Street, North Windham, Boody's in background
Courtesy of Windham Historical Society

Anapolis Oct 12 1861

Dear Mother I will now
try to answer your letter
I was very glad to hear
from home & to hear how
well father was getting
along with his falls work
we have been here about 4 days
we dont know how long we shall stay
at this place you mentioned Wm
Stevens you said somthing about
his pass he run away from
Augusta the day we was mustered
into the service he did not get
any pass or furlough he run away
with about half A Dosen more
of the same stamp I shall get an
honerable discharge or else I shall
stay till the war is ended before

Then conquer we must,
When our cause it is just
And this be our motto—
"IN GOD IS OUR TRUST"

Joseph's handwriting
Courtesy David Manchester

81

Postage due letter to Nahum; notice upper left hand corner reads
"Soldier's Letter"

Cotton, a novelty item for Joseph's family
Courtesy David Manchester

Stand by the Flag.

THE FLAG OF LIBERTY.

1776. 1861.

THE
FATHER
OF HIS
COUNTRY
LEFT THIS
TO HIS
CHILDREN.

Patriotic embossing on Joseph's stationery

Baseball game at Fort Pulaski, Georgia; Company G;
48th New York Volunteers are in the foreground.
Courtesy of National Park Service, Fort Pulaski National Monument, Georgia

Fort Pulaski, 2012
Courtesy David Manchester

Views of Fort Clinch, Fernandina, Florida 2012
Courtesy David Manchester

Fort Sumter in silhouette
Courtesy David Manchester

Interior view of Fort Sumter, north end of Morris Island in the distance
Courtesy David Manchester

Landscape of Folly Island
Courtesy David Manchester

General Hospital #2, circa 1862
Library of Congress photo, Courtesy of Stephen Wise

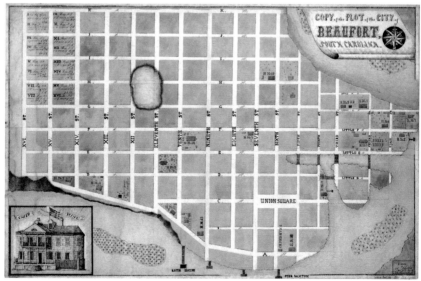

Beaufort, SC map with hopsital sites, circa 1862
Library of Congress photo, Courtesy of Stephen Wise

2012 side view of residence used as General Hospital # 2
Courtesy David Manchester

Front view of residence used as General Hospital # 2
Courtesy David Manchester

Joseph's stone in Arlington Cemetery
Courtesy David Manchester

Joseph's stone at Beaufort National Cemetery; Union stones have
rounded crowns and names are framed within the shield
Courtesy David Manchester

David Manchester by the gravestone of his great uncle, Joseph K. Manchester
Courtesy Carol Manchester

Beaufort National Cemetery
Courtesy David Manchester

Maine soldiers' stones
Courtesy David Manchester

Confederate soldier's stone; Confederate stones have a chevron apex
Courtesy David Manchester

Chapter 12

BEAUFORT

Prior to the Civil War, Beaufort was a center of culture and affluence in the American South. Immense fortunes were made through the cultivation of rice, indigo, and, later, greatly prized sea cotton. Wealthy plantation owners built breathtaking residences in Beaufort, where they could benefit from cool breezes coming off the river. The town was also a hotbed of secessionist sentiment.

As the Federal fleet circled Port Royal Sound, Beaufort was among the settlements in the area targeted in the Port Royal campaign and captured on November 7, 1861. Learning that the battle for the islands and coastal area soon would be lost, most wealthy residents fled, abandoning mansions, homes, plantations, fields, cotton stores, slaves, and gardens to the victors. Beaufort would remain occupied by Federal forces for the rest of the war. Homes were confiscated but not destroyed. Rather, they were used by the Union for headquarters, officers' residences, military storage, hospitals, and similar employ. As a result, much of Beaufort's historic antebellum beauty remained after the war, and subsequent preservation ordinances in the twentieth century have perpetuated many of Beaufort's significant and extraordinary Civil War structures.

Unaware that Joseph lay in a Beaufort hospital with the shoulder wound inflicted during the July 18th Battery Wagner charge, Seward and Lydia were penning their letters to Joseph on July 26, and she had prepared a package for him with the requested knitted socks and some of her homemade candies.

North Windham July 26, 1863 [a Sunday evening]
Joseph, I have just returned from the Graffams. Robert
starts tomorrow. He will bring you a few things; one pair of socks

is all I can send. I will send another pair soon as I get them done. I want to know if you are coming home on furlough. Send us word when you write again. I have sent you some ink, a bunch of envelopes, two pounds of sugar, a little of peppermint wrapt in a white hankerchief, some pieces of old cloth. You can use them for any purpose you please. Where do you get towels? I will send some if you want them. When I send another box I think you will laugh when you see the little box sent this time. I heard Robert had gone till your father saw him one day last week. He don't offense like his brother. He seems like somebody. We like him very much. It is getting late in the evening. I would tell you about the drafted men but Robert knows all about them. I wish the state of things was under martial law. Too many of the union men are gone. The copperheads are overpowering us. If they are not looked after they will do mischief. I wish you could hear the boldness they use in renouncing the government. Such language ought to be stopt and would be if we could have our way. Be a good boy and write often. Israel Boody says he wants you to write to him and tell him all about the battle. He wants something he can believe. The papers contradict themselves sometimes. Good night for the present. L D Manchester

July 26, 1863
Dear Brother Joseph, I seat myself to answer your last letter which I received the other week. I was very glad to hear that you was well and hope these few lines will find you the same. We are all well at home. Robert Graffin leaves here tomorrow morning to go out whare you be. We are getting along well with our work. We have got oar hoeing all done. We have got about half of oar hay in. I am going to send you some papers if I can get them. Forgive bad writing and mistakes. Seward

Just as Joseph's letters reflected the news of the day and his opinions of it, so does this letter from his mother, the only surviving letter to Joseph from her which was found among the letters in the farmhouse. Evident are the similarities to her son's style, expressions, and command of language in the way she shares the local news and offers her views;

both like to write in lists and both share a deep sense of patriotism. Their epistolary conversations are of like mind. Evident also is her affection for him, read between the lines and in the package she has prepared to send to him.

Seward likewise has been trained in the letter writing conventions of the day, beginning with the familiar "seat myself to answer" and concluding with "Forgive bad writing and mistakes." It would have been a comfort to Joseph to know that the hoeing was all done and half the hay was in.

A letter dated July 30, 1863, from Moses and addressed to his niece arrives in Windham around early August. It is written from Hilton Head, South Carolina, and is optimistic despite its announcement to the family of Joseph's having been wounded.

> *Dear friend Rebecca,*
> *I have not time to rite mutch so you must excuse me. I have heard from Joseph. He got wounded in the fight at Moris Island and he is in the Hosbittle at Bufort. But he is not woundid bad. A ball went through his arm. He will git out in a short time and then I think he will come home. Answer this as soon as you git it. Direct to Hilton Head Boat Yard.*
> *Yours in Haste, Moses Austin*

Moses is writing from Hilton Head Boat Yard, and in an earlier letter Joseph had written that Moses was a carpenter. Below, Stephen Wise describes the military activity on Hilton Head in August, 1863, and Moses' probable job.

> At Hilton Head was located a vast engineer depot which provided finished products that were brought to Morris and Folly islands. This included items made of iron and cut board lumber that was manufactured at steam-powered sawmills. The completed items were then placed on board quartermaster vessels that kept up a constant shuttle between Hilton Head and the islands off Charleston.[1]

One sawmill, no doubt, was the one taken from St. Mary's in November, 1862.

Chapter 13

DEATH

The next notice about Joseph comes from Rapheal Sanford and, with the exception of punctuation and initial capital letters, is presented here as Mr. Sanford wrote it. One hundred fifty years later it can still evoke tender emotion. The Edward Means house in historic Beaufort was used as General Hospital No. 2 and still stands.

> *General Hospital No 2*
> *Beaufort, S.C. Aug. 20, 1863*
> *Dear friends,*
>
> *It is with a sad heart that I set down to write your family about your son which was brot to this Hospital the 19th of July wounded thrue his right sholdir. We thought that he would git up in a few days. He lingered a long for searl days and then the Dr. cut it opend and took out Sumbomb which was brokend. Then he got a long for searl days till the mortafication set in. Now my Dear friends mastr your hart for the cumen strugal which you must pas thrue and put your trust in him that giveth taketh away. After five days of sufring your son dreft slowly away and dide and now he fils a Soldier's grave and a rued bord marks the plas in S.C. for his bed plas whare he lays with thousands of soldiers around him. Weap not for he lost his life fiting for god and his Country.*
>
> *He was chistently bured with the stars and strips proudly flatin above him. He was loved by all that new him. I know that his peas was with god. So chear up and bleas as he bleased and mak your peas with god and think every Soldier out to be*

pearpared for this grat chang.

I got a leter from your brother and your leter was in it. He has gave to his regment so I thought I would mak so bold as to write to you. You. must escus all mistakes and for speling for I huried to write__army. Pleas next tym put on your dricktons for I hardly new where to write to. I am a nurse in this Hospital and have attended meny a dying bd sid but never as hard as this.

Pleas to write let me now whether you got this leter or not. Drickt to Mr. Rapheal G. Sanford General Hospital No. 2 Beaufort S.C..... Your brother did not cum her to sea him. This plas is 15 or 16 mils from hilton head. I shall write to your brother. Pleas write, in post from your friend R.G.S.

Much of Sanford's letter is readable. However, to accommodate some of the peculiar wording or spelling, the nurse's letter is presented again in more familiar form. His natural poetic phrasing is particularly noteworthy.

Dear friends,

It is with a sad heart that I set down to write your family about your son which was brought to this Hospital the 19th of July wounded through his right shoulder. We thought that he would get up in a few days. He lingered along for several days and then the Dr. cut it open and took out something which was broken. Then he got along for several days till the mortification set in. Now my Dear friends, master your heart for the coming struggle which you must pass through and put your trust in him that giveth [and] taketh away. After five days of suffering your son drifted slowly away and died and now he fills a Soldier's grave and a rude [simple] board marks the place in S.C. for his bed place where he lays with thousands of soldiers around him. Weep not, for he lost his life fighting for God and his Country.

He was Christianly buried with the stars and stripes proudly flatin [flattened] above him [or more conventionally, with a flag laid upon his casket]. He was loved by all that knew him. I know that his peace was with God. So cheer up and bless as he blessed and make your peace with God and think every Soldier ought to be prepared for this great change.

I got a letter from your brother and your letter was in it. He has given it to his regiment so I thought I would make so bold as to write to you. You must excuse all mistakes and for spelling for I hurried to write__army. Please next time put on your directions [as in Direct to] for I hardly knew where to write to. I am a nurse in this hospital and have attended many a dying bedside but never as hard as this.

Please write to let me know whether you got this letter or not. Direct to Mr. Rapheal G. Sanford, General Hospital No. 2, Beaufort S.C.... Your brother did not come here to see him. This place is 15 or 16 miles from Hilton Head. I shall write to your brother. Please write, in post from your friend R.G.S.

Beaufort National Cemetery was among the first of six national cemeteries authorized by President Lincoln in 1863 for the purpose of reinterment of soldiers and sailors who had died in the region. It also was the final resting place for men who died in nearby Union hospitals during the occupation, and many of the men who lost their lives at Battery Wagner during the July 1863 siege are buried here. According to military records, Joseph died at General Hospital No. 2 around 5 p.m. on August 3. Having Joseph's body preserved and transported home was a prohibitive expense for the poor family, and, consequently, Joseph was buried where he died. He was interred on or about August 4 at Beaufort National Cemetery, and since Joseph died at a local hospital, the grave very likely is his original burial site, according to cemetery representative Louis N. Brown. In a conversation in 2012, Brown noted that the granite headstone would have been placed within a few months to replace the "rude board" that functioned as a temporary place holder for the stone. Final resting place for almost two hundred Confederate soldiers, Beaufort National Cemetery is distinguished as the only national cemetery containing Confederate soldiers. It is also the serene and beautifully landscaped home for row upon row of unknown soldiers.

Certainly the letter brought immense sorrow to the Manchesters, who likely anticipated that Joseph, though wounded, would recover and return to them; and yet, Nahum and his family to some extent were fortunate ones. At least Nahum and Lydia knew their son had been given medical care, such as it was in 1863, nursing attention, comfort, and a respectful burial. They had closure while so many other men died in battle and were hastily covered with dirt on the battlefield or perished in prisons. Too often, information about their demise made it back to family only if a buddy scribbled a note off or if some identifying element—a letter, a photo, or a paper information tag on the soldier found later on the body—might provide a source for communication with the family.

Sanford's letter is inspiring for its genuine, heartfelt simplicity and inherent desire to console. He comforts the family by relating how much others liked Joseph, that Joseph has his peace with God, that he had the burial of a Christian and a patriot, and that Joseph's dying was difficult for Sanford personally. He speaks of courage and honor: "Weep not for he lost his life fighting for God and his Country." Joseph died sixteen days after being wounded.

Sanford's written record informs of other important details. Although Joseph was transported by steamer to the hospital within hours of the battle, several days transpired before a doctor sought to remove the bullet fragment(s). Gangrene was the likely "mortification."

Sanford alludes also to a letter that Moses had forwarded for Joseph, thereby determining the Windham mailing address. It is reasonably assumed that the forwarded letter is Lydia's of July 26 and that Joseph never read it. In later correspondence from Moses, he writes that he is returning her letter along with Joseph's things. It is through this circuitous route that the only extant letter from Lydia to Joseph remains.

Despite his attempt to comfort Lydia, Moses's own sense of loss is touchingly evident in this next letter to his sister.

> *August 23, 1863   Hilton Head, S.C.*
>
> *The mail has not left yet so I will rite the particulars about Joseph. He was shot in his rite shoulder and it mortified which was the cause of his death. The last time I saw him was at St. Hellena before the fight. He came to me and told me he had no money to git paper with. He said he wanted to rite home. I gave him fifty cents to git some with. At that time he had a gold watch. He paid 60 dollars for [it]. He said he should carry it home if he lived to go. Since that, he was paid of, but I cannot find out anything about his watch or money. He died in the Hosbittle at*

Bufort. He rote to me at the boat yard that he was in the hosbittle wounded. [This sentence may explain his writing to Rebecca on July 30th that he expected Joseph would be all right.] *I got his letter and answered it. And the next day I heard he was dead. I could hardly believe it when I heard it. But it is so. The poor boy is in Heaven and you should none of you mourn for him. He is happy in Heaven. He died a brave souldier in the defence of his country. Dear friends, I am left alone out here and I feel lonesome since Joseph died and I hope you won't forgit me. I do not know as I have got any friends since Joseph died and I will go to Bufort as soon as I can and see about his cloths and send them to you by express, and I will try to find out about his money and watch.*

My dear friends, I will close by telling you not to mourn for Joseph for he is happy and let him rest. Do not forget to rite to me. Direct your letters like this: to Moses Austin, Hilton Head S.C. 9th Maine Regt, Co K.

Organized in June, 1861, to promote clean and healthful conditions in Union army camps and to provide supplies, raise money, and staff field locations with nursing volunteers, the Sanitary Commission eventually emerged as a point of contact and clearinghouse for families in their efforts to discover information regarding wounded, slain, or missing sons, husbands, fathers, brothers, and loved ones.

Since to this point, all Nahum had received were letters from the Beaufort Hospital nurse and his brother-in-law Moses, Nahum sought official confirmation. The terse and perfunctory reply from the Sanitary Commission appears below.

Sanitary Commission,
Central Office, 244 F Street
Washington, D.C.

August 31st 1863
Sir,

In reply to your inquiry respecting Joseph K Manchester of 9 Rgt Maine I am sorry to inform you of the dead above named.

He died at Beaufort S.C. August 3rd [18]63
    Respectfully
    John Bowne
    Supt Hosp Dis[Unreadable]
North Manchester Esq
North Windham Me.

Two things about this response suggest that it was penned by an amanuensis for John Bowne. Below Bowne's title is unreadable script looking very much to be a name, as if another person wrote the response for John Bowne. Moreover, if such is the case, the writer may already have written several of these form responses that day because inattention shows *North* where the name *Nahum* should have been in the address closure.

Fortunate it was that Joseph's parents had Moses to see to Joseph's belongings and money and to provide details. Communication continues from Moses on September 20, 1863. On this date he was writing from Morris Island, which finally had been abandoned by the Confederates on September 7. Sea bun is another term for sea urchin.

> *Dear Sister, I have sent Joseph's cloths to Portland.... You will find them at Adams Express office in Portland. You must see to it immediately or His cloths will shoil in the box. You Will see a coat of mine in that box; in the pocket is a white hancherchief and a Sea Bun. Keep it safe for me until I come home.*
>
> *There is some things of Joseph's which I have not found. As soon as I find them I will send them to you. The note on the gold watch I paid/30 dollars. The note was 50 fifty dollars. Joseph paid 20 dollars. Dear friends, you must not forgit me because Joseph is dead, but I hope I shall live to return to tell you the whole story about Joseph. I cannot express it to you now, but if I live to git home it will be a great satisfaction to you to hear the truth of things about Joseph in regard to his company. After Capt Shaw was killed and Liet Brieks was wounded Lieut Beul was in command. He treated him like a rascal, but he was not with them. Sorry. I have had a fight with Beul a number of times because he crowed on Joseph. But he never could with me nor no*

*other man in that company. Rite every Sunday to me and direct
to Hilton Head, Moris Island Boat Yard. Moses Austin*

Also from Moses, undated but a few days later, arrives another note; he is quite anxious about the box, his coat, and his handkerchief. His concern invites questions. Had he sent home a sum of money wrapped in the handkerchief in the pocket? Was the "sea bun" (which would deteriorate) an indirect way of advising Lydia to look for money?

> *Dear Sister, you will find Joseph's things at Adams Express
> office in North Windham or Portland. The box is directed to
> Nahum Manchester North Windham Maine.... In that box is a
> new coat which is mine. Take good care of it for me. There is more
> that belongs to Joseph but I have not got yet. Take this receipt
> with you to the office.... Answer this and let me know if you git
> the box.*
>
> *Remember the coat that has got the white hancherchief in
> the pocket is mine. You take it and keep it for me until I come
> home and I will make you a present. The rest are Joseph's things.
> Keep that coat safe and you will oblige your brother.*

In the meantime, Nahum has contacted Rapheal Sanford, the thoughtful nurse at General Hospital No. 2, who replied on October 9, 1863. The letter below maintains his original spelling and style. The handwriting in this letter is faint and at times undecipherable.

> *Dear Sir:*
> *I resead* [received] *your letttr a few days ago and now
> hasten to answer it. I am well and hope you are enjoying the same
> blessing. You spok of a whatch and pen. They are heir but the Dr
> will not ford them without an order from his captain for if he
> shuld, the captain mint make him truble. Now the way for you
> to do it is to wright an letter to the Comandr of Company K. Tell
> shot at Moris Island and have him send an order to a C Benedict
> and he will send them to the Captain and the Captain will send
> them to you. You see that is a safe way. Then the Capt can't keep
> them all. The Drections you want is Comander, Co K, 9 Me ...*

Moris Island S.C. and the watch will go. Now friends I want to [k]now if being a stranger mad any difrant to me about doing my duty and [k]now I mad ... the same to any one. What a grat duty rests on me to close the eyelids of sum of my companions most eary day. Yesterday thir was 7 diad and thir is 3 or 4 in this hospital all most ready to depart from this wicked world. It maks me feal bad to sea so many pase a way but it is Gods will that it is, so if I am called a way from this world thank God I am ready but still I wood rether dye whir my friends had look over and watch me but then I don't [k]now as it maks any difrant whir one dys if his chart is Gods. What a warning it is to us soldiers to sea so meny of our companions pas a way. I do not now whether your son was a Christian or not but I nevr heird him swar. We have got an nise bauring ground heir with white bords with regiment and Co and age and your son lays ... grave in the yard. I shall have sum roas bushes put thir. Now kind friends I will with your blessing and Gods I will all was try to do my duty to God and my Country. Today thay opened on to Charlston and thir is one [unreadable] and probably by the next mail thir will be other sad new and of sum [unreadable] but may God halp thou to bear this strogle. If I can git home I will try and cum and see you. I will tell you wher I live when I am to home. I live in Camden, Oneida County [unreadable] and [unreadable] may now unreadable].
Be sure to Wright to the Captain. Now may God bless and keap you till I heir from you again.

> *I remain your humble servant Rapheal G. Sanford*
> *Wright ... and excus all mistaks.*

People demonstrate character through their words and deeds, and Sanford's letter shows him to be very cautious, perhaps suspicious, but also thoughtful and helpful. Concerning Joseph's watch, he acknowledges that it is at the hospital and, in an effort to assure it is not lost in the chain of custody, suggests documentation by getting an order from the captain for its release.

> *They are here but the Dr will not forward them without an order from his captain for if he should, the captain might make*

him trouble. Now the way for you to do it is to write a letter to
the Commander of Company K. Tell [him that Joseph was] *shot*
at Morris Island and have him send an order to a C. Benedict
and he will send them to the Captain and the Captain will send
them to you. You see that is a safe way. Then the Capt. can't keep
them all.

He is a good hearted man and asks if even though he is a stranger,
he has made a difference by writing to Nahum and Lydia. Administering
to the wounded and dying with heartfelt care, certainly true in Joseph's
case, this nurse recognizes his vast responsibility with deep emotion. He
exhibits personal patriotism as well as a belief in God, and is prepared
when he himself is called.

> *What a great duty rests on me to close the eyelids of some*
> *of my companions most every day. Yesterday there was 7 died and*
> *there is 3 or 4 in this hospital almost ready to depart from this*
> *wicked world. It makes me feel bad to see so many pass a way but*
> *it is God's will that it is.*

Since the battles are ongoing and Sanford daily sees fellow soldiers
dying, he is somewhat philosophical in this letter.

> *So if I am called away from this world, thank God I am*
> *ready; but still I would rather die where my friends can look over*
> *and watch me but then I don't know as it makes any difference*
> *where one dies if his chart is God's. What a warning it is to us*
> *soldiers to see so many of our companions pass away.*

Joseph's character similarly is indicated by what Sanford says about
him.

> *I do not know whether your son was a Christian or not but*
> *I never heard him swear. We have got a nice burying ground here*
> *with white boards with regiment and Co and age and your son*
> *lays __ grave in the yard. I shall have some __ bushes put there.*
Clearly Sanford held Joseph in high regard.

> *Now kind friends, I will with your blessing and God's I will*
> *always try to do my duty to God and my Country.*

He closes with what he hopes will be some hopeful news: *Today*
they opened onto Charleston;

awareness that there will be more soldiers brought in: *and probably*
by the next mail there will be other sad news;

words of sympathy: *but may God help thou to bear this struggle;*

the possibility of meeting Joseph's family: *If I can get home I will try*
and come and see you. I will tell you where I live when I am to home. I live
in Camden, Oneida County;

a reminder: *be sure to write to the captain;*

and a benediction: *Now may God bless and keep you till I hear from*
you again.

Rapheal Sanford, nineteen years old, was a member of the 81st Infantry Regiment, New York, Company E. His unit would leave the Beaufort area in the autumn of 1863 and Sanford would be killed at the battle
of Cold Harbor, Virginia, on June 3, 1864.[1]

Chapter 14

MOSES

Morris Island, October 23, 1863—from Moses Austin

The information about Joseph's watch stands out particularly in this letter as does Moses's doubt that the money Forest Higgins collected ever was sent. Like Rapheal Sanford, Moses too would like to believe his efforts are appreciated. "For if I live" has become a common theme in mail bound for North Windham.

> *Dear Brother and Sister, I received a letter from you stating that you received that express bill. Now I want to know if you got the box containing his letter. I spoke to you about my coat. I want you to keep it safe, for if I live to come home I shall know where to find it. My coat had a white hankerchief in the pocket. You spoke about that watch. I sent the note to you that I took it. Joseph bought the watch for gold but I found that it was nothing but brass cases marked with gold. Therefore I got rid of it as quick as I could to get my 30 dollars back. It was not worth 20 dollars what Joseph had paid. But there was $8.80 cts in money that Forist Higgins collected of the boys that owed Joseph. He said he put it in a letter and sent it to Beaufort. After Joseph was buried there and I wrote to the Post Master and doctor and they wrote to me that no such letter had ever been there, I do think that Higgins kept that money. I cannot git any information about it. But a man that will rob a poor dead boy will do anything. I have done the best I could for him and you. I shall go to Beaufort soon and see where he is laid and I shall put a grave stone at his head. But I must close. Answer this and tell me if you git the box. Direct to*

Morris Island Boatyard In the care of Capt Burns Q M [Quarter Master].

Moses's next letter, also from Morris Island, is written November 5, 1863. Ever the helpful brother, he wants to know how much his sister had to pay for freight on the box of items he had sent. A conversation about their parents follows. *Lydia, you wanted to know what I thought about going to Iowa to see father and Mother. I will go with you.*

The rest of the November 5 letter:

> *I sent five dollars to Mother and she got it. One of their neighbor's rite to me that Ebben and his wife did not treat them well and he said they had not got cloths to keep them warm this winter. Ebben has treated them in a shameful manner and he never will prosper.*

The Eben of whom Moses writes is their brother Ebenezer, who is in Iowa. Census records indicate that the parents of Lydia and Moses resided with Eben and his wife.

> *I have no news to rite. I suppose you git more news than I do. I have ben sick but I am getting better. They tel us that we are to bee discharged the first of June next and I hope we shal for 3 years is a long time to stay from all of our friends.*

Moses has been at Morris Island since September 20, 1863. Though he writes in a later letter that he has written about once a week, no other letters were found at the farmhouse dating from the four months that intervene between the November 5 letter and this next one, dated March 11, 1864. He seems dispirited and terribly lonesome, but, as always, very generous.

> *Dear friend Rebecca, It has ben a long time since you have rote to me and I suppose that you do not think anough of me to take the trobble to rite a line to me. Rebecca I shal never rite another to you until you rite to me. Since Joseph died I am out here*

without any friends but I thought I had some friends at home, but I think I have not got any. If I had I should hear from them once in six months. I have one person that rites to me once a week but it is a person that I never saw. But I like to read letters from the North from any one that will rite to me. Mary has never roate to me. I made up my mind to make you and Mary a handsome present if I live to git home, and if you would like to go to Iowa with your mother and I, you can go. I will pay your fare if you want to go and see the folks [Rebecca's maternal grandparents]. *My time will soon be out the 22d of September. The officers tel us that we shal bee discharged the 13ᵗʰ of July but I do not think so.*

Rebecca pleas answer this letter if you never rite to me again. Yours with respect, Moses Austin.

And on the same paper:

Dear Sister and Brother, I will rite a line to you. I suppose you have seen the Strout boys [Estes and Nathan]. *They are at home on a furlow and I heard that they all went into Augusta in Disgrace. They were all Drunk and I am glad that I was not with them. They have got to come back and stay 3 years more, and when I come I shal come for good. I want you and Nahum to rite. I have no news to rite you so I will close. So good by. Be shure and answer this.*

This next letter is the last of Moses's letters that were found in the Manchester farmhouse. It was dated March 24, 1864, two weeks later.

Dear Brother and Sister, This day I received a letter from you stateing that Ebben [their brother] *was dead, and it is the first letter I have had from you for a long time. I have answered all of your letters and I should bee happy to answer more if I could git them. I rote to Rebecca and had no answer yet, but if I live I shal bee at home in six months. I have not mutch news to rite except Disserters are coming into our lines vary often. I should like to have rite often for I should like to hear from you. Lydia, you tel Rebecca to take some cloth of the same kind of my* coat and cover the Buttons and I will send her the money to pay her if she will do it. I will send her a dollar. If she can not do it, you do it and I will send it to you. Let me know about it in your next letter.

But I will close with my best respects to you all from Moses Austin. Direct to Morris Island Boat yard SC in care of Capt. Burns Quarter Master. Good Knight.

Chapter 15

PENSION

Joseph's story does not end with his death, however, for the years following his death continued to be emotionally and financially difficult for Nahum and Lydia. Not only would they lose Joseph in 1863 but their daughter Emily would die in 1869 and Mary would follow two years later. Additionally, a few adversarial neighbors stymied Lydia's claim for the pension to which she was entitled as mother of a deceased soldier, one who also had been dependent upon him.

With Joseph's death, Henry showed greater awareness of his parents' need, and in November, 1864, Henry wrote of sending his parents $75. The draft will specify on it *"to be payed in United States gold coin."*

In June, 1865, Henry wrote that he wanted to know how they are situated, *"all about good or bad. I want to know the whole. I know you have had to work hard all of your life and I am well aware that you have ever tried to do what was for the best."*

Applying for pension benefits on October 1, 1866, Lydia signed a declaration under oath. The survivors' benefits were based on the Pension Act of July 14, 1862:

> Sec. 3. … shall hereafter die, by reason of any wound received or disease contracted while in the service of the United Sates, and in the line of duty, and has not left or shall not leave a widow nor legitimate child, but has left or shall leave a mother who was dependent upon him for support, in whole or in part, the mother shall be entitled to receive the same pension as such officer or other person would have been entitled to had he been totally disabled; which pension shall commence from the death of the officer or other person dying as aforesaid: *Provided, how-*

ever, That if such mother shall herself be in receipt of a pension as a widow, in virtue of the provisions of the second section of this act, in that case no pension or allowance shall be granted to her on account of her son, unless she gives up the other pension or allowance: *And provided, further,* That nothing herein shall be so construed as to entitle the mother of an officer or other person dying, as aforesaid, to more than one pension at the same time under the provisions of this act.

Lydia also had to declare that she had "not in any way been engaged in or aided or abetted, the rebellion in the United States."[1] Lydia qualified.

Copies of deeds show son Henry holding a mortgage on the Windham farmhouse and land since 1857, and H. H. Boody holding what may have been a second mortgage or note in 1867 for Nahum's accumulating debt. Boody owned a grocery, and an affidavit of his in the pension files states that "before enlistment the soldier was employed as a farmer at a pay of $15 per month and board and he gave the greater part of his wages to the applicant for support. For two years prior to enlistment the soldier was regularly in the habit of purchasing groceries of for his mother's use; that after entering service he sent his mother the greater part of his wages regularly from time to time."[2] They had been very much dependent upon Joseph.

In further support of her need were the following statements, taken from the summary of Joseph's pension file.

"H.H. and Israel Boody, October 22, 1866. 'The real and personal property of the applicant does not exceed $75 and they know of their own personal knowledge for two years prior to the soldier's death the applicant was in part dependent on him.'

"Capt. Coleman Harding, October 22, 1866. Capt. Harding testifies that soldier was a member of his company and was always in the habit of sending to his mother a part of his army pay regularly from the time he entered the service until his death of which facts he has personal knowledge, that the soldier has or did give affiant money to forward to the applicant.

"Capt. Thomas E. Wentworth, October 22, 1866. Testifies

that soldier gave him money which he delivered to applicant." [3]

Also in support of her record of need was a Windham town abstract from the treasurer's 1862 books for the "Allotment," the money that Joseph had arranged for his father to receive in Windham for a while.

The pension claim was allowed on the foregoing evidence, noted as having been filed October 22, 1866, together with proof of service and death of the soldier. But within a year the pension was suspended and on October 12, 1868, Lydia reapplied. Her affidavit follows in part:

> "That owing to the false statements of my personal enemy the payment of my pension was suspended.
>
> "I further depose and say that the real estate and personal property of myself, and of my husband Nahum Manchester does not exceed the sum of two hundred dollars.
>
> "That the farm upon which I reside is mortgaged to Henry H. Boody and Henry L. Buck. [Henry L. Buck is a clerical error; Henry Buck Manchester, the son, held the mortgage on the property. The affidavit is not written in Lydia's hand.]
>
> "That said mortgage is liable to be foreclosed at any time. That myself or my husband Nahum Manchester have no means of any kind to pay said mortgage on the farm on which I reside.
>
> "That my husband Nahum Manchester is old, and owing to sickness, is unable to perform little or any manual labor, for my support.
>
> "That I am dependent on my pension for support.
>
> "That as evidence of the truth of the foregoing I offer the annexed affidavit." [4]

The personal enemy to whom she refers is Levi Tobie, who filed a number of letters between 1867 and 1871 against her claim. In them he charged that Lydia did not warrant the pension "on the grounds that the family owns more property, pays more taxes, and the husband does more work than the average man young or old." [5]

Concerning the husband's ability to "do more work than the average man young or old," however, D. O. Perry, MD, the Portland area examining surgeon in pension cases, filed in his October 19, 1868, report that "after thorough, minute, and careful examination of Nahum Manchester ... I have found evidence of the following diseses, injuries & disabilities, namely:

1. Chronic Inflammation of the Liver of long standing.
2. Irritation in the kidnies and bladder, attended by pain, tenderness over these organs, & frequent calls to pass urine.
3. Left wrist, arm & shoulder nearly useless for manual labor, by reason of for[mer] injuries.
4. Right knee in the habit of slipping out of joint, by reason of former injury of a violent character.
5. Left foot has been cut in four different places, thus compelling him to walk on the outside of the foot.
6. The little finger of the left hand is dislocated, & has never been reduced & is therefore not only useless, but in the way.

In consequence of these, he is able to do very little manual labor."[6]

Lydia's pension was reinstated but suspended a second time in 1870, upon the representations of Levi Tobie, E. H. Mayo, and a remonstrance signed by 29 others and filed on August 29, 1870,[7] who instigated that "the soldier was never main dependence of family as his parents own a farm of 75 or 80 acres and have 3 other boys, one of whom now lives at home and they have oxen, cows, sheep, and a good horse and a husband is as able bodied a man as they know."[8] Seward, then 20, was the only son living at home.

However, in consequence of later evidence, a medical statement filed on May 6, 1871, and the town assessor's statement filed on May 27, the suspension was lifted in June.[9] Dr. Abraham Anderson, MD, had attested to disease of kidneys and irritation of bladder from which Nahum, 65 years old, could never recover.

In the years that Tobie was writing his letters, the seventy-acre farm had been mortgaged since 1857 to Henry in Washington Territory for eight hundred dollars. In his 1873 report, a special agent summarizes that Nahum "pays no interest on the debt further than the taxes on the place ... and that he was making improvements in and about the house. Claimant showed a letter from son in W.T. dated April 6, 1870 requesting that the farm on which he held the mortgage should be sold."[10]

Complaints as to the fraudulence of the claim yet <u>again</u> surfaced, the cause investigated, and Lydia Manchester once more was dropped from the rolls, based on the report of the agent and the opinion of the Medical Ref A (report). That examination of Nahum implied that he was neither seriously incapacitated nor unable to support his family.

> Special agent certifies that he examined the claimant's husband and found him 68 years old, color fresh and good, whole appearance that of a healthy laboring man, looking in better health and condition than most men of his age for labor. Pulse 76, full and strong, tongue clearance healthy, walks a little lame from a cut many years ago in the metatarsal joint of great toe of left foot. The joint projects inwardly about an inch. Shoe of that foot does not show that he is obliged to walk on the outer side of his foot to any great extent. "It is run down" somewhat but the sole is worn very evenly. He has several corns between the toes which in my opinion causes more lameness than the wound. The little finger of the left hand has been injured so that when opened it stands away from the ring finger at an angle of 35 degrees but it has good grasp when shut. He says that sometimes the knee joint floating cartilage slips out of joint and troubles him, complains also of being compelled to urinate a quantity making but little water at the time and also of pains in the upper region which are more severe when hungry.[11]

A few Windham cronies of Levi Tobie also had been drummed up to testify on October 2, 1873, that Nahum was capable of arduous, physical work:

> … has known the family for forty years, has worked with husband lumbering and have allways considered him a healthy rugged man. Last winter he cut and hauled wood all the time which I know because I hauled wood on same road nearly all winter and was in the habit of travelling the same road with him…
>
> have always regarded him as able to support his family by his labor as well as the majority of small farming in the neigh-

borhood...

have inspected town accounts and find that claimant and her husband pay more than the average per capita in the school district, which is one of the largest in town.[12]

In February, 1880, Lydia filed "a statement signed by 30 citizens including selectmen of Windham, Maine setting forth that in their opinion the applicant had been made a victim of political persecution and that her name was dropped on representation of political enemies of the applicant's husband." Included was John Fellows's statement showing abatement of the assessor's poll tax for Nahum "on account of physical disability."[13]

Also in February, 1880, "Ephraim R. Brown, Deputy Sheriff of Cumberland County Maine, testified that he was with the special agent in September or October, 1874 as near as he could recollect the date, when he took the testimony of Staples and Mayo above, and that at the time of his taking their testimony the witnesses were both intoxicated. He added that Staples has not to his knowledge lived in the state since July, 1877 and is reported to have absconded to avoid criminal prosecution for forgery."[14]

Undoubtedly, most persuasive of all, however, was the testimony of Cyrus Parker and Frederick Legrow regarding Levi Tobie. Their statement follows:

It is a matter of <u>common report</u> in Windham that Nahum Manchester and Tobey have had a personal quarrel for ten years or more, said to be a political quarrel. On or about December 7th 1878, in the morning at the door of Frank Boody we were all present with Tobey and others. Conversation was then and there made between Tobey and others present during which Tobey declared that he had felt called upon to take steps to stop the Manchester pension because he and Nahum had a business transaction years ago in which Tobey stated Manchester had cheated him out of six hundred or seven hundred dollars. When asked whether he considered this now as having seen justice done, he replied that he was able to sleep better at night now that the pension was stopped and that if an attempt was made to restore the pension he would go on foot to Washington to stop it if necessary. He said he had derived a good deal of satisfaction and felt well paid for all the trouble he has been to in getting the pension stopped.[15]

In a reversal of just deserts, Levi Tobie's gloating cost him. At last, in March, 1880, Lydia recovered the $8 per month pension due her, uninterrupted until her death on December 7, 1898.[16]

Next to Lydia and Nahum in Arlington Cemetery in Windham are Alice, Emily, and Mary. The monument inscribed with Emily's name also lists Joseph's name, company, regiment, and date of death following the battle at Fort Wagner, Morris Island. It is this monument and Joseph's letters that led David Manchester and his family to learn more about this ancestral great uncle.

Chapter 16

EPILOGUE

FORT WAGNER

Often obscured by larger events and battles during the Civil War, the fierce struggle and terrible defeat for Union control of Morris Island and Battery Wagner in July nonetheless led to an important outcome. The exceptional courage of the 54th Massachusetts black troops under Col. Robert Gould Shaw against hopeless odds raised military confidence in their commitment, abilities, and success, thereby furthering much needed additional recruitment. Determined to own this position so important to the blockading of Charleston Harbor, the Union initiated siege operations, whereby once again African-American soldiers drew praise for their willingness and endurance in the hazardous fatigue duty. On September 7, 1863, Confederate forces abandoned Fort Wagner under cover of night after almost two months more of heavy naval bombardment.

Devised of logs, earthworks, and sandbags, Battery Wagner eroded over time as winds and hurricanes hauled it off to sea, and today it is under water; although some portions of Morris Island still exist, they are reachable only by watercraft.

FAMILY, FRIENDS, AND THE WINDHAM BOYS

In 1862 Eben enlisted in the Civil War, joining the 20th Maine as a wagoner. Eventually he yielded to Henry's invitations, for Eben appears as a laborer in Castle Nook on the Washington State and Territorial Census of 1878; however, *Chronology of Great Falls 1764 – 1934* reveals that by 1884 he and his family had established their home and lived in North Gorham, Maine, where he became involved as an agent for Nason's School. He died of Bright's disease in 1911.

One of the earliest letters from Henry Manchester was written in September, 1859, from Washington Territory. He held several jobs but the one at Puget Mill Company, Teekalet, in the territory netted him a substantial income as a young man. After learning of Joseph's enlistment he wrote home November 23, 1861.

> *I received a letter from you to day and was very glad to hear you informd me that Joseph had gorn to the war. I feel very sory to have him go but he has gorn in a good corse. I cannot [help] feeling proud of him for in all the accounts that I have read of the war he is the only Representitive of the whole Manchester name there. It is I suppose very hard for you to part with him, but should it be his lot to fall by the wicked hands of the traitors their is one thing he will have to console him. That is that he died in a good corse that defending his contry, that contry which every American has to. And let me tell you as a words of conciliation that I think he has the same God to protect him there that he would have at home.*

Henry's letter intended to comfort, no doubt. It must be mentioned also that as the war wore on, several Manchester family members did serve. Henry's brother Eben enlisted in the 20th Maine in 1862, and Dole records an Edward Manchester in light artillery. Dole also records that Joseph's uncle, Stephen, served with light artillery in the Wilderness campaign and Stephen's son, Greenleaf H. Manchester, died in 1864. Paul E. Little, a family member by marriage, was wounded at Chancellorsville and died in a hospital in July, 1863. These men are but a few of the kin who fought for the Union.

More than twenty of Henry's letters are among the family papers, and occasionally he mentioned coming home; however, nothing of record indicates that he did. He married Ellen Brownfield when he was about thirty-two years old and remained in Washington for the rest of his life to live and raise his family. Henry died in 1891.

Short of her appearance on the census records of 1850 and 1860 showing that she was living at home, no other record about Rebecca has yet been found. From the many cajoling sentences and pleas from Joseph, Moses, and Henry to hear from her, it is evident she was not a very dedicated correspondent.

Within fifteen years Lydia and Nahum would lose four of the younger children: Joseph, at Morris Island in 1863, age twenty-one; Emily in 1869, age twenty-three; Mary (Chaffin) in 1871, age thirty-two, and Alice in 1878, age thirty years. The 1870 census lists Mary and Orin living in Massachusetts, and their son Frank Chaffin as part of Lydia and Nahum's household.

Joseph's friend Almon Freeman, brother to Sargent, and Joseph's second cousins Albert and Royal Manchester, were listed on the Civil War draft registration records of 1863–1865. None served. Dole writes:

> July 17th 1863, the government ordered conscription and Windham's quota was 69 men. Of these, none entered the service. The town voted to raise the money and hire substitutes which was accordingly done. 24 furnished substitutes of themselves; 28 were exempted for physical disability; and 17 for other causes; but the town's quota was filled.[1]

"The Ninth Maine, Company K Windham boys"[2]

November 1, 1861	Sargent Freeman died of illness at Fort Monroe, Virginia.[3]
April 2, 1863	Joseph's Fifth Maine, Company A, Windham friend Almon Shaw died from disease contracted in the service.[4]
July 11, 1863	Stephen Libby died in the initial attempt to take Fort Wagner on Morris Island.[5]
July 17, 1863	Amos H. Hanson also was killed at Morris Island.[6] He had enlisted on September 21, 1861, as a musician.
December 5, 1863	George Nason died in St. Augustine, Florida, of disease contracted in the service.[7]
August 9, 1864	Frank Morton died of wounds received in battle on June 15, 1864, at Petersburg, Virginia.[8]

Both Albert Graffam and Warren Howe were promoted to full corporal and mustered out in the summer of 1865.[9]

Charles E. Morton, James Small, and Estes Strout mustered out in September, 1864, after fulfilling their three-year commitments.[10]

Nathan A. Strout was discharged for wounds on January 26, 1865, and on the same day married Ellen Meguire in Windham, Maine. After her death in 1873, he married her sister Etta in Conway, New Hampshire.[11]

Elbridge Libby lived a long life in Windham, dying of stomach cancer at the age of 81.[12]

The Austin uncles, Moses and Benjamin, were members of Joseph's 9th Maine regiment, Company K, and had signed up on September 21, 1861, with Joseph. Already in their forties at the time, they found the war hard on their bodies. Moses suffered from chronic rheumatism for the rest of his life and was in and out of Togus, the disabled veterans' home, several times. He no longer appeared on the Togus record after September, 1883. Benjamin was admitted to Togus in August of 1888 with his disability listed as old age and varicose veins. Records suggest that he died a month or two later.[13]

Forest Higgins, the fellow who wrote to Nahum and Lydia about Joseph's mumps and whom Moses believed had kept the money he had collected following Joseph's death, eventually was promoted to full first sergeant.[14] Beginning in 1908, he too spent time periodically at Togus with heart-valve difficulty and a history of rheumatism. He died in Bangor in 1914.[15]

By 1873, Lydia and Nahum were in their late sixties and Seward, now twenty-two, remained the only offspring living at home. The others had married and established residences and families of their own or had already died. For Nahum, who still had a farm to manage, it seemed logical and reasonable that he and Lydia should deed the homestead and acreage to their youngest son Seward and on June 6, 1873 they did. "In consideration of the maintenance of me Lydia D. Manchester and Nahum Manchester my husband, with good support, meat, drink, clothing, lodging and all other necessities suitable for persons of our age and condition during the whole of our lives paid by Seward M. Manchester of Windham, County of Cumberland and State of Maine (If the above consideration is fulfilled) the receipt whereof I do hereby acknowledge, do hereby give, grant, bargain, sell and convey unto the said Seward M. Manchester, his heirs and assigns forever a certain piece or parcel of land situated in Windham...."

The deed's language about providing for the parents as the conveying price is not surprising for it should be noted that Lydia was in the midst of her pension difficulties, which did not resolve until 1880. Two years later Seward married Ida Frances Nason and in the farmhouse in which he grew up he raised his own four children.

Seward also continued to learn, as his older brother Joseph often advised in his letters.

A farmer, in time Seward became an inventor and businessman as well. On February 8, 1890, he and Charles Wentworth applied for and received a patent for "improvement of creaming cans," the improvement being a design for better separation of cream from milk. Employing agents and using express shipping, they sold the "Eclipse" creaming can through the 1890s.

Additionally, in 1892, Seward inquired of Chase and Son in Portland about an engine to run his shingle mill, and a letter of interest from John McClure of "Westbrook City" for lumber to build a house appears in the record in 1894. Lumber, which long had been a means for the Manchester income stream, developed from harvesting to milling and sales. Civic minded like so many of his family, he was the census taker for Windham in 1900. When Seward died in 1904, he was buried in the old section of the cemetery, about 260 feet away from his parents and siblings.

APPENDIX A

John Stevens Cabot Abbott, a Brunswick, Maine, native born in 1805, was a Bowdoin College classmate of Henry Wadsworth Longfellow and Nathaniel Hawthorne, class of 1825. Like the stories and poetry of his writer-friends, his 1866 account of Fort Wagner during mid-July 1863 is a literary rather than historical effort. Still, the excerpts below are interesting for their representation of the literary style of the period and of the war.

They are taken from his book, *History of the Civil War comprising a full and impartial account of the Origin and Progress of the Rebellions, of the various Naval and Military Engagements, of the Heroic Deeds Performed by Armies and Individuals, and of Touching Scenes in the field, the Camp, the Hospital, and the Cabin Vo. II*, pages 326–329.

July 10th … the ironclads were running up along the shore, and about nine o'clock they opened fire upon Fort Wagner, eliciting a vigorous though harmless response. The bombardment continued for several hours without much damage being inflicted by either party. Admiral Dahlgren, who had succeeded Admiral Dupont as commander-in-chief of the naval force, was on the Catskill, which was struck fifty-two times. The only damage she suffered was in the driving back of a bolt, which just grazed the admiral's head, inflicting however no injury. The troops bivouacked for the night among the hillocks of the marshy island, having made preparation to storm the forts the next morning.

With the early light of the 11th, the Seventh Connecticut, supported by the Ninth Maine and the Seventh Pennsylvania, moved noiselessly along the shore shrouded in the dim twilight of the morning. Unobserved, they pressed on until the enemy's pickets were encountered, who gave the alarm. A terrible fire was instantly opened upon the advancing patriots. With a shout they rushed headlong into the storm of bursting shells, hand grenades, and rifle-balls, which were hurled upon them. The darkness was however such that the rebel gunners could not take good aim, and comparatively few were struck down. Not a man flinched. On they rushed, over obstructions into ditches, treading upon torpedoes, until they clambered the parapet and sprang into the works. A hand-to-hand contest of great desperation was now waged. The rebels were gradually driven behind such protections as the interior of the ramparts afforded. The Seventh Connecticut led in this heroic charge.

The Seventy-sixth Pennsylvania pressed on close behind. But in the increasing light the rebels had got a better range, and they were exposed to a more destructive fire.... Again they rushed in through such a staggering tempest of mutilation and death, that but few reached the parapet. The Ninth Maine, seeing how matters stood, and that it was impossible with the force they had to carry works which were proved to be so strong, commenced a retreat. The Connecticut troops, with the few from Pennsylvania who had joined them, were now in an appalling condition. Every moment they were falling before the unerring rifles of the foe. Their commander was severely wounded, and no reinforcements could come to their aid. It was impossible for them without support to hold the works into which they had plunged. A retreat was of necessity ordered. It became a fearful race for life. The rebels turned their guns, charged with grape and canister, upon them, and the patriots fell in dreadful slaughter.

During the interim of the next seven days "the rebels were strengthening their works, the patriots were busy throwing up intrenchments that they might permanently hold the ground which they had gained "

Upon the 18th, a new attack was make [sic] on Fort Wagner. It was first assailed by a fierce bombardment from the iron-clad gunboats Montauk, Ironsides, Catskill, Nantucket, Wee-hawken, and Patapsco. These boats took position within short range of the fort, while several wooden gunboats at a greater distance, pitched their shells into the ramparts of the foe.... From noon till night the bombardment raged sublimely. It, however, accomplished but little. The beauty of the parapet was destroyed. The defensive power of the fort was not, however, materially weakened.

At sunset the fleet withdrew, and the cannonade ceased. Just then a black cloud appeared in the sky, with muttering thunder. One of the fiercest of tempests commenced its roar, as if to show how insignificant the artillery of earth compared with that of the skies. In the midst of this storm, preparations were made to carry the fort by assault. Three brigades, under charge of General Strong, Colonel Putnam, and General Stevenson, were brought forward for the perilous enterprise. To a thoughtful mind the plan did not give promise of success. The brigades were hurriedly at the moment formed for the duty. The troops were but very imperfectly acquainted with their brigade commanders. Many had never before been under fire; and all remembered the bloody repulse of the 11th.

The evening twilight was fading away, when these troops with solemn tread moved along the hard beach, from which the tide had retired, to the assault. Colonel Shaw, at the head of the Fifty-fourth Massachusetts colored troops, led. These were followed by the Sixth Connecticut, under Colonel Chatfield, the Forty-eighth New York, under Colonel Barton, the Third New Hampshire, under Colonel Jackson, the Seventy-sixth Pennsylvania, and the Ninth Maine, under Colonel Emory. These troops were to march half a mile over the smooth, hard beach, in direct view of the enemy, and exposed every step to the murderous fire of his guns. By point blank range the batteries of Wagner could sweep this beach with grape and canister. At the same time, the barbette guns on Fort Sumter and the heavy batteries on Cummings's Point could rake the line with an enfilading fire. Never were men doomed to a more terrible storm of iron hail.

As they, with rapid step, commenced their march, instantly the terrible tornado of war burst upon them. Leaving their path strewed with the dead and dying, they rushed on, breasting the smothering tempest, till, plunging through he ditches and clambering the parapet, they engaged in hand-to-hand fight with their foes. The ditches were raked with grape and canister from the rebel howitzers. Hand grenades and every other murderous implement of war fell mercilessly upon them. Patriot and rebel fought with the utmost desperation. There has been no conflict during the war in which the Union troops displayed more heroism. Never did men fight with death staring them more steadfastly in the face. The famous charge at Balaklava was scarcely more desperate.

The imagination can hardly conceive a scene more awful than was now presented. It was night, and a night of blackness of darkness. The earth seemed to shake beneath the terrific peals of thunder, while vivid flashes of lightning frequently illumined the spectacle with their terrible glare. Sulphurous clouds of smoke hung over the struggling combatants, while the cries of onset and the explosions of artillery and musketry were blended with the awful roar.

The carnage was dreadful. In a few moments, General Strong, Colonel Shaw, Colonel Chatfield, Colonel Barton, Colonel Green, Colonel Jackson, and a large number of brave officers, had fallen. The Fifty-fourth Massachusetts Colored Regiment, having lost their revered commander Colonel Shaw, performed prodigies of valor, and fought with heroism, which was for them the love of nation, under their surviving youthful leader, Lieutenant Higginson. The patriot troops forced their way into a corner of the fort, and, for an hour, held it. The fort was too numerous in its garrison and too strong in its works to be thus taken. It was madness to remain longer under so deadly a fire. The order to retreat was given. It required desperate valor to fight their way into the fort. It required no less valor to fight their way out again. Over a thousand rebels had reposed quietly in their bomb-proofs unharmed by the bombardment, and, the moment our charging columns appeared, rushed out fresh for the fight.

It was midnight when our troops retired, still exposed, as they retreated along the beach, to the pitiless peltings of this battle-storm. The expanse was covered with the wounded, the dying, and the dead. Twinkling lights were seen here and there, as friendly hands sought the wounded and bore them, in stretchers, from the range of fire. Some, their life-blood ebbing away, fell sweetly asleep, as with placid smile they dreamed of those friends and that home which they would never see again. Others, in the frenzy of delirium, shouted and sang, while the music of the tireless billows chanted funeral dirges all along the desolate shore.

Joseph Manchester

Sunrise Chart
Tuesday, March 15, 1842
Windham Center, Maine
Tropical Placidus True Node

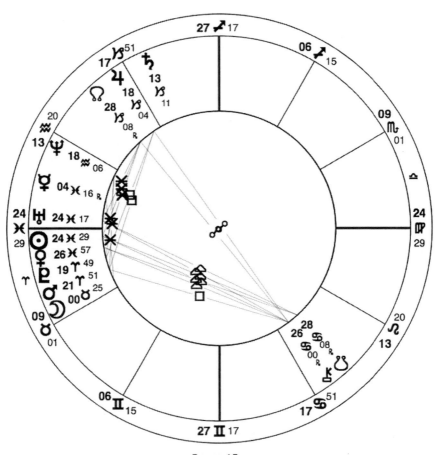

Prepared By:
Beth Guy
15 Martin Road
Portland Maine 04103

APPENDIX B

Discovering how Joseph's astrological chart may have resonated with his life's path has been an interest of mine for a while and is offered here with a discussion of several planetary influences for those who share a similar curiosity. To astrologer Beth Guy for her generous gift of time and interpretation, this author owes a great debt.

Obviously it is easier to "forecast" after the fact and that surely is true of Joseph's astrological chart. Further, because his time of birth is unknown, the chart may be inaccurate with regard to planetary/house placement. Even so, it is thought-provoking to look at the planetary associations in Joseph's chart, in this case using sunrise as the determining "birth time," to see what basic themes emerge.

Worthy of immediate notice is that Joseph's South Node (the horseshoe glyph) is in Cancer, a nurturing sign, and its placement fits with wanting to take care of the parents and of his attachment to home and family. Throughout his letters Joseph wrote of wishing he could help with the work on the farm and of sending home money. He frequently inquired of his parents' overall well being.

Joseph was born on March 15, 1842 and thus has a Sun in Pisces. As a planetary sign, the Sun is an evolutionary path, a process of self-actualization. His Sun conjunct[1] Venus speaks to a personal charm while the Sun conjunct Uranus suggests eccentricity or intuition. Those with a sign in Pisces generally are compassionate, imaginative, and self-sacrificing. Their basic nature is that of the mystic. Compassion and sacrifice are specific words here that readily associate with Joseph.

An observation of major significance is that he has a stellium[2] in Pisces (Uranus, Sun, Venus, and Mercury), which is quite powerful, and as a consequence, there can be a great deal of intuition or psychic attunement. Joseph may have had strong intuitive concerns about the upcoming battle of July 18 when he wrote that *I may be shot in battle.* Then again, he just may have been facing reality.

The Moon represents feelings and emotion. It symbolizes the part of consciousness that is sensitive to its surroundings. Based on the sunrise casting of this chart, Joseph's Moon placement is in Taurus, a sign of determination, persistence, and intuition. Again, intuition shows up. Joseph does appear likeable, determined, and persistent, with a strong desire to excel, certainly to succeed. Thus, his Moon in Taurus seems a good call.

Beth Guy noted further that "if he had been born prior to sunrise, he'd have Moon in Aries, which could have conjuncted Mars/Pluto. That's definitely some warrior spirit and desire to live life 'on the edge.'"

Additionally, "the Pluto/Mars in Aries conjunction [itself] is very powerful. What's very interesting is that Aries and Pisces are markedly different energies and he has a powerhouse of both — the Warrior (fiery dynamics) and the Mystic (watery passivity)."

The just-can't-miss observation in Joseph's chart is that *all* of his planetary influences fall within four consecutive houses and while the 10th, 11th, 12th, and 1st houses may not be *the* actual house placements, it is telling that the planets will fall consecutively in four houses somewhere. Assuming that Joseph *was* born around sunrise, those nine planets and the Sun fall on the left side of the chart or, in astrological language, in the Eastern Hemisphere. This is the ascendant. This is the sunrise. This is the dawn of another day with new opportunity and hope. For Joseph, the Union's position was his position, a unified country. Joseph's letters suggest a continued optimism and hopefulness.

In her summary, Beth Guy observed that "Joseph has Chiron[3] (wounded healer) conjunct the South Node in Cancer. Chiron also trines that Pisces stellium and squares the Aries conjunction.... He identifies with the country's wound (Cancer Chiron) and tries to help heal it through being a warrior and a risk-taker (difficult conflict/battle—Aries) and does so, in a sense, through sacrifice and compassion (Pisces).... Chiron in Cancer probably contributed also to emotional sensitivity and attunement to the suffering of others." Otherwise stated, Joseph is able to put his strong sense of duty (Jupiter and Saturn in Capricorn) to the country (Cancer is the natal sign associated with the U.S.) as a warrior (Mars/Pluto conjunction in Aries) into a spiritual perspective (the four planet stellium in Pisces). He may have brought courage to others in a quiet way.

Certainly, knowing Joseph's time of birth would enable a more detailed and complete astrological reading. Still, with respect to this overview of Joseph's natal astrological chart, coupled with the knowing of Joseph through his letters, his picture of the sky on March 15, 1842, invites thoughtful consideration of the journey Joseph was meant to take. Moreover, this snapshot picture in time portends the optimism, courage, and patriotic sensibility that destined Joseph to enter the Civil War and to give up his life for his belief in it.

NOTES

YOUTH

1. Samuel Thomas Dole, *Windham in the Past*, ed. Frederick Howard Dole (Auburn, ME: Merrill & Webber Company, 1916), p. 37.
2. "Joseph K. Manchester Pension Papers," National Archives, Washington, D.C. (hereafter listed as JKM papers).
3. JKM papers.
4. JKM papers.

ENLISTMENT

WASHINGTON, D.C.

1. Frederick Henry Dyer, *A Compendium of the War of the Rebellion* (Des Moines, IA: Dyer Publishing Company, 1908), p. 1222.

ANNAPOLIS

COATZACOALCOS

1. William C. Lowe, "Battle of Port Royal: Account of the Battle of Port Royal, An Eastern Theater Civil War Battle During the American Civil War," *America's Civil War*, January 2001. Used with permission of Weider History Group.
2. Ibid.
3. Ibid.
4. Ibid.
5. Historic Fort Monroe is a national monument in Virginia.
6. Dole, p. 268.

7. Lowe, "Battle."

PORT ROYAL and the SEA ISLANDS

1. Lowe, "Battle." This battle pitted Thomas F. Drayton against his Union brother, Commodore Percival Drayton, who commanded naval forces against Confederate forts.
2. Lieutenant Aaron H. Chase, "History of Company H, 9th Maine Volunteer Infantry," ed. Rick Hagen, March 9, 2011, www.kinquest.com/usgenealogy/civilwar/9thMaine.php.
3. Hurricane Number 8—November 1861.
4. Lowe, "Battle."
5. Chase, "History."
6. While he doesn't mention the fort by name, it is likely that Joseph is at Fort Walker.
7. A 1924 obituary clipping found among family papers states that Royal Manchester was "acknowledged the best known dancing master and violinist in the State." Royal had begun playing publicly at dances when he was 15.
8. Almon Shaw died of disease contracted in the service, April 2, 1863. Dole, p. 268.
9. Henry B. Manchester, letter to parents, January 21, 1862.

FERNANDINA

1. Chase, "History."
2. "A Guide to Fort Pulaski," Fort Pulaski National Monument, Georgia, U.S. Department of the Interior: National Park Service, 2011. Courtesy of Fort Pulaski National Monument.
3. Ibid.
4. Dyer, p. 1222.
5. Nahum had hired George Woodbury, who performed "most of the work and in fact all except light chores and jobbing." JKM papers.
6. Chase, "History."
7. Ibid.
8. George H. Nason died of disease contracted in the service in the hospital at St. Augustine, FL, December 5, 1863. Dole, p. 268.

HILTON HEAD

1. Dyer, p. 1222.
2. Stephen R. Wise, *Gate of Hell, Campaign for Charleston Harbor, 1863* (Columbia, SC: University of South Carolina Press, 1994), p. 57.
3. Ibid.

ST. HELENA

1. Wise, p. 57.
2. Ibid., p. 29.
3. Abraham C. Myers, quartermaster-general of the Confederate States; Jefferson Davis, president of the Confederate States of America; Pierre Gustave Toutant Beauregard, Confederate general and in command of South Carolina, Georgia, and Florida during the time Joseph was there; John B. Floyd, brigadier general in Confederate army.
4. Wise, p. 52.
5. Ibid., p. 53.
6. Ibid., p. 48.
7. Ibid., p. 53.
8. Ibid.
9. Ibid., p. 43.

FOLLY ISLAND

1. Wise, p. 228.
2. Ibid., p. 61.
3. Ibid., p. 64.
4. Ibid., p. 65.
5. Ibid., p. 68.
6. Ibid., p. 69.
7. Ibid., p. 70.
8. Ibid., p. 229.
9. Dole, p. 268.
10. Wise, p. 86.
11. Ibid., pp. 95–96.

BATTERY WAGNER, MORRIS ISLAND
1. Wise, p. 103.
2. Ibid., p. 107.
3. Ibid.
4. Ibid.
5. Ibid., p. 233.
6. Ibid., p. 232.
7. Ibid., p. 233.
8. Ibid., p. 113.
9. Ibid.

BEAUFORT
1. Wise, p. 143.

DEATH
1. U.S. Civil War Soldier Records and Profiles.

MOSES

PENSION
1. JKM papers.
2. JKM papers.
3. JKM papers.
4. JKM papers.
5. JKM papers.
6. JKM papers.
7. JKM papers.
8. JKM papers.
9. JKM papers.
10. JKM papers.
11. JKM papers.
12. JKM papers.
13. JKM papers.
14. JKM papers.
15. JKM papers.
16. JKM papers.

EPILOGUE
1. Dole, p. 267.
2. Dole, p. 261.
3. Dole, p. 268.
4. Ibid.
5. Ibid.
6. Ibid.
7. Ibid.
8. Ibid.
9. U.S. Civil War Soldier Records and Profiles.
10. Ibid.
11. Ibid.; Maine Marriage Records, 1705–1922; New Hampshire Records Index, 1637–1947.
12. Maine, Death Records, 1617–1922.
13. U.S. National Homes for Disabled Volunteer Soldiers, 1866–1938.
14. U.S. Civil War Soldier Records and Profiles.
15. U.S. National Homes for Disabled Volunteer Soldiers, 1866–1938.

APPENDIX A

APPENDIX B
1. In astrological terms, a conjunction is a line-up of two (or more) planets within three degrees of each other. In astronomy, a conjunction is perceived as a direct or nearly direct line up of planets.
2. A stellium comprises three or more planets in the same sign or house, and because of that concentration, the house, or in this case the sign, can dominate Joseph's experience.
3. Chiron is the K with the small rectangle below it.

BIBLIOGRAPHY

"A Guide to Fort Pulaski." U.S. Department of the Interior: National Park Service. Fort Pulaski National Monument, Georgia, 2011.

Abbott, John C. *History of the Civil War: Comprising a Full and Impartial Account of the Origin and Progress of the Rebellions, of the Various Naval and Military Engagements, of the Heroic Deeds Performed by Armies and Individuals, and of Touching Scenes in the Field, the Camp, the Hospital, and the Cabin, Vol. II*. Springfield, MA: Gerdon Bill, 1866.

"Baseball at Fort Pulaski National Monument." National Park Service post card.

Bradshaw, Timothy E., Jr. *Battery Wagner: The Siege, the Men Who Fought, and the Casualties*. Columbia, SC: Palmetto Historical Works, 1993.

Chase, Aaron H., Lieutenant. "History of Company H, 9th Maine Volunteer Infantry": Ed. Rick Hagen, http://www.kinquest.com/usgenealogy/civilwar/9thMaine.php.

Dyer, Frederick Henry. *A Compendium of the War of the Rebellion*. Des Moines, IA: Dyer Publishing Co., 1908. (Reprinted 1959, NY: Sagamore Press; Thomas Yoseloff.)

Dole, Samuel Thomas. *Windham in the Past*. Ed. Frederick Howard

Dole. Auburn, ME: Merrill & Webber Company, 1916. (Reprinted 1974, Windham Historical Society.)

Faust, Drew Gilpin. *This Republic of Suffering, Death and the American Civil War*. New York: Vintage Books, 2008.

Goodwin, Doris Kearns. *Team of Rivals: The Political Genius of Abraham Lincoln*. New York: Simon & Schuster, 2005.

Hurricane Number 8—November 1861: http://www.aoml.noaa.gov/ hrd/hurdat/ easyread- 2010.html.

Kozak, Ginne. *Eve of Emancipation: The Union Occupation of Beaufort and the Sea Islands,* 2nd edition. Beaufort, SC: Portsmouth House Press, 1996.

Lowe, William C. "Battle of Port Royal: Account of the Battle of Port Royal, an Eastern Theater Civil War Battle During the American Civil War." *America's Civil War.* January 2001.

Maine Death Records, 1617–1922.

Maine Marriage Records, 1705–1922.

National Archives, Washington, DC: Joseph K. Manchester Pension Papers.

New Hampshire Records Index, 1637–1947.

Scholl, Josephine Manchester. *Chronology of Great Falls 1764–1934,* 1985.

Soldier, Kay. *Memories of Windham.*

U.S. Civil War Soldier Records and Profiles.

U.S. National Homes for Disabled Volunteer Soldiers, 1866–1938.

Wise, Stephen R. *Gate of Hell, Campaign for Charleston Harbor, 1863.* Columbia, SC: University of South Carolina Press, 1994.

Letters—1861 to 1864

Joseph K. Manchester to parents Nahum and Lydia, sisters Rebecca, Mary, Emily, and Alice, and brother Seward

Henry B. Manchester to parents Nahum and Lydia

Moses Austin to sister Lydia Manchester and niece Rebecca Manchester

Rapheal G. Sanford, nurse at Hospital No. 2, Beaufort, SC, to Nahum and Lydia Manchester

Sanitary Commission Superintendent John Bowne to Nahum Manchester